More
From the Quarries
of
Last Chance Gulch
Volume 2

D1566422

JON AXLINE
ELLEN BAUMLER
CHERE JIUSTO
LEANNE KURTZ
HARRIETT C. MELOY
KIMBERLY MORRISON
VIVIAN A. PALADIN
RICHARD B. ROEDER
DAVE WALTER

HELENA
INDEPENDENT RECORD

Bruce Whittenberg, Publisher

DEDICATED
TO THE MEMORY OF RICHARD B. ROEDER

ISBN 1-56037-115-3

Prepared for publication by
American & World Geographic Publishing

Contents

INTRODUCTION

"The excavation of Helena's history will continue," predicted Dave Walter and the late Richard B. Roeder in their introduction to the first volume of *More From the Quarries of Last Chance Gulch,* published in 1995. They were right.

The well-illustrated series of weekly historical studies, written by a group of able and dedicated writers, researchers and historians, began appearing in March 1994, in the *Independent-Record.* The series was launched by Associate Editor Dave Shors who envisioned a modern continuation of the research done by the late William C. Campbell, long-time member of the *Independent Record* editorial staff. Campbell's work resulted in two books entitled *From the Quarries of Last Chance Gulch,* published in 1951 and 1964. Although regrettably not indexed, the books have long been prized by researchers and general readers alike, and today, copies are hard to find.

It is fitting that the new series was named *More From the Quarries of Last Chance Gulch,* not only to honor the work of Bill Campbell but also to suggest and encourage its continuation. The original core group of writers, Jon Axline, Ellen Baumler, Chere Jiusto, Leanne Kurtz, Harriett C. Meloy, Richard B. Roeder and Dave Walter, began contributing articles so well done and so well received that their first compilation in book form was soon underway. Now in 1996, a second volume appears, and it is likely more will follow.

This writer, pleased to join the group in 1995, welcomes this opportunity, in an introduction to Volume II, to express some commendations for work well done and to make a sincere confession: I did not know as much about the history of this wonderful town and its environs as I thought I did.

There were topics I knew something about, but not in significant depth. A case in point: "James Whitlatch and the Last Chance Motherlode" by Kim Morrison, another newcomer to the list of contributors. There are many other instances that could be cited here, and all of them are included in these pages.

Aside from the courteous, helpful leadership of Dave Shors in launching and perpetuating the series, there is Ellen Baumler. Not only does she consistently contribute interesting and well-researched articles on many subjects, but she continues to "ramrod" the schedules, keeping everyone well informed about deadlines, photo possibilities, even doing some legwork for someone who has been out of harness for a number of years. Her contributions to this volume include an article about the steamboat *Fern,* whose singular voyage between Townsend and Great Falls proved why Fort Benton was the head of navigation on the Missouri River.

Two former colleagues of mine at the Montana Historical Society have been a particular joy to encounter via *Quarries.* They are, of course, Harriett Meloy and Dave Walter, who have been contributors from the beginning.

Harriett has reacquainted us with Helen Clarke, the half-Indian daughter of Malcolm Clarke, a fur trader who established a stage station at what is now the Sieben ranch north of Helena in 1864 and was murdered there by angry members of his wife's family in 1869. Helen Clarke waged her own battle for recognition and acceptance and emerged, finally, as an "unsung heroine." Among Harriett's other subjects was Lizzie Fisk, wife of editor Robert Fisk of the *Helena Herald.* Mrs. Fisk's letters to her family "back east" reveal her enthusiasms about her new home in Montana but also some deep racial and social prejudices, common to people of her time and station, but distressing to most of us today. Finally, in a special section devoted to the destructive earthquakes that struck Helena in October 1935, Harriett tells her own experiences as a teenager, seeking, with the help of her date for the evening, to find out if her family was safe.

Dave Walter, a favorite with every one of us who have sought to know about the history of Helena and indeed beyond the borders of Montana, is equally a favorite *Quarries* contributor, although like this writer, he has inadvertently stepped on some sensitive toes a time or two. His articles about the gangster era spawned by Prohibition in the 1930s and the bizarre "woman in white" murder story elicited some protestations from descendants of those concerned.

In my case, criticism was evoked when I indicated I was in agreement with most authorities that the first gold in paying quantities, beyond "colors," was found by the discoverers of Last Chance Gulch near the Colwell building in mid-July 1864, not at the site of the Montana Club at the corner of Sixth and Fuller. One reader called to say he knew where the big find was, and it was not at the Montana Club *or* the Colwell building site, but close to the entrance leading to the Norwest Bank's drive-up teller windows and ATM.

Along with Ellen Baumler, the State Historic Preservation Office has been the home base for two other excellent contributors to the series, Chere Jiusto and Leanne Kurtz. Chere began making her mark in 1976, when she launched her study of Helena's oldest neighborhoods, and produced an excellent guide to those places. Her article about the original Canyon Ferry, now a place for power generation and recreation but once the connection between Helena to the gold fields in the Belt Mountains, is in this volume as is her study of Helena's location on an unpredictable earthquake fault. The latter is an important part of this book's look at the last time, over sixty years ago, that this fault wreaked destruction and death in the Helena area, and the real probability that it will happen again.

Leanne Kurtz is responsible for a number of provocative articles on subjects ranging from Coxey's Army, the story of desperate unemployed men during the 1890s depression who sought to find relief by marching to Washington, to the history of East Helena's Asarco smelter. Leanne also contributed to the earthquake story.

Jon Axline, historian for the Montana Department of Transportation, writes about many subjects, but most reflect his interest in mining and transportation. In this volume, he deals with the Empire Mine and Mill, which had a deep impact on the Marysville mining district, and the transportation, mining and agricultural history of the Little Prickly Pear Valley. Jon also deals with the ghostly history of a "haunted house" on "Central" Avenue in Helena. Axline adds a general history of the 1935 earthquakes.

Finally, we have the last contributions of Richard B. Roeder, the New Englander who became one of Montana's best known historians. At the time of his death two days before Christmas in 1995, Rich still had many historical irons in the fire, articles to write, experiences to share. It is appropriate that this volume is dedicated to him.

In the issue of February 15, 1996, a Thursday, editor Shors used the familiar *More From the Quarries of Last Chance Gulch* logo, together with Dr. Roeder's picture, and published a series of tributes, written by colleagues, most of them fellow contributors to *Quarries*.

Rich Roeder's final articles, published in this book, deal with Thomas J. Walsh, one of Montana's truly great politicians, and, appropriately enough, the Montana Historical Society, his favorite place for research and intellectual nourishment during his years in Helena.

Rich Roeder was one professional historian who became convinced that researching and writing about one's community with searching accuracy but without footnotes and other academic trappings is a worthy pursuit, one that transcends any wish to add to one's *vita* sheet. When the harvest of those writings is compiled in a well-illustrated and well-organized book, it becomes an entertaining and informative treasure worthy of the shelf of any home or institutional library. Rich Roeder and Dave Walter were right: the carpet of Helena's history is not threadbare but has a very "deep pile" indeed. Probing its depths for more treasures will continue.

Vivian A. Paladin
Helena, Montana
June 1996

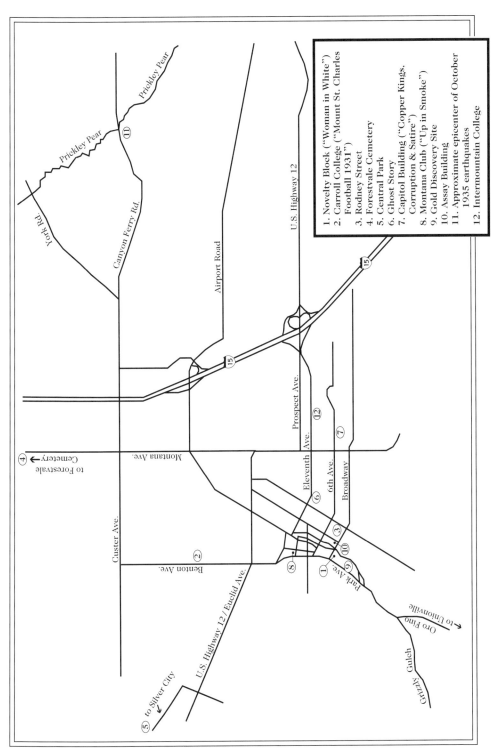

1. Novelty Block ("Woman in White")
2. Carroll College ("Mount St. Charles Football 1931")
3. Rodney Street
4. Forestvale Cemetery
5. Central Park
6. Ghost Story
7. Capitol Building ("Copper Kings, Corruption & Satire")
8. Montana Club ("Up in Smoke")
9. Gold Discovery Site
10. Assay Building
11. Approximate epicenter of October 1935 earthquakes
12. Intermountain College

Prickley Pear

Prickley Pear

York Rd.

Canyon Ferry Rd.

Airport Road

U.S. Highway 12

U.S. Highway 12 / Euclid Ave.

to Silver City

Custer Ave.

Benton Ave.

Montana Ave.

Prospect Ave.

Eleventh Ave.

6th Ave.

Broadway

Park Ave.

Oro Fino

to Unionville

Grizzly Gulch

to Forestvale Cemetery

9

PEOPLE

Montana Historical Society's Early Years

BY RICHARD B. ROEDER

What is the oldest history organization in the trans-Mississippi West? What agency holds 95 percent of all the newspapers ever published in Montana? What is Montana's oldest state agency, founded in 1865? What agency is the largest repository of official state and territorial publications? What state agency conducts a history conference that is the most well-attended such conference in the United States? What agency publishes a historical journal that has the largest circulation in the country? What state agency controls the largest collection of C.M. Russell paintings in the United States? If you answered "Montana Historical Society" to all of the above, you know your historical beans.

The Historical Society is one of Helena's and the state's greatest cultural resources. Its museum displays attract thousands of visitors, and its library of 100,000 volumes, unmatched newspaper collection, and over 300,000 photographic images make it a mecca for amateur historians, genealogists, and scholars from around the country.

The 1865 Territorial Legislature passed an act of incorporation that recognized a group of twelve male corporators, among whom were the earliest white arrivals in Montana, as the "Historical Society" in order to "collect and arrange facts in regard to the early history of this Territory." This was essentially a private club of limited purpose headed by its early and perennial president, Wilbur F. Sanders. Since its beginning, the story of the Society has been one of evolution from a private club to a public agency that performs functions of government as well as providing services for the general public.

While the earliest years saw limited accomplishments, the existence of the Historical Society was the product of impulses of people similar to those we characterize as "civilizers," that is to say, individuals who saw themselves as participating in the creation of a new civilized community as well as pursuing individual wealth. It was this same impulse that led forward-looking citizens to support early education and to assume leading roles in the creation of Yellowstone Park. It was this same concern for the collective future that caused some early Montanans, with Helenans among them, to record past achievements as spurs to future acts of good citizenship.

During the first few years the Society experienced limited success in gathering materials, but beginning in the early 1970s, it became more active and underwent incremental changes that transformed it from a private club into a public agency. Early in 1874 members moved their collection from Virginia City to Helena, where it was housed in the law offices of Wilbur F. Sanders. The move was just in time for the collection to be wiped out in the fire of January 9, 1874, one of a series of fires that destroyed downtown Helena. Society members had to rebuild their holdings, and in doing so, they appealed to the public for support.

The move to Helena also seems to have been a sign of a reinvigoration that aroused public awareness and legislative intervention. An act of May 7, 1873, provided a small appropriation from the legislature. That same year the Society wrote a constitution which, among other things, provided for new categories of membership. One new category was corresponding members. Undismayed by limited progress and remoteness, the group elected as corresponding members such nationally famous historians as George Bancroft and Francis Parkman, whose popularity made them celebrities of national stature.

The constitution also provided for the office of librarian who would remain the principal administrator until the legislature created the office of director in 1951. The reinvigorated group also produced the first volume of the Society's *Contributions* in 1876. It was a collection of journals and reminiscences covering the years 1863-1874. It would be another 20 years before the second volume would appear, but in all, the

Contributions would total 10 volumes with the latest appearing in 1940.

As the Society grew, it increasingly relied on the legislature for help. In 1883 it got another small appropriation. By 1887 the Society's collection of books, newspapers, and memorabilia, now open for public use, required more space. The legislature supplied money to rent rooms in the Lewis and Clark County Courthouse. It also appropriated a small sum for the librarian's salary.

In 1891 the legislature changed the name to the "Historical Society of the State of Montana" and declared that the agency was a trustee of the state and made an appropriation for the librarian's salary. It placed the governance of the agency in a five-member board of trustees appointed by the governor and made the governor, secretary of state, and attorney general ex officio members of the executive committee. In 1898 Laura Howey became librarian. Howey was the first librarian with library experience and supplied vigorous leadership in collecting materials and appealing to the legislature for financial support. In 1902 in an act of symbolic significance, Howey moved the library to rooms in the newly-created capitol. By these acts the transition from a private club to a full-blown state agency was more or less complete.

During its early and most uncertain years, the name of Wilbur F. Sanders was synonymous with the Historical Society. Like most civilizers, Sanders engaged in myriad civic activities in addition to an important law practice. A prominent Mason, Sanders is probably best remembered for his prosecution of George Ives and organization of the Vigilantes. He served four terms in the territorial legislature as a representative from Helena. He was a perennial unsuccessful Republican candidate for territorial delegate to Congress and a delegate to numerous national Republican Party conventions. When Montana was admitted to statehood, he was one of the first two U.S. senators elected by the legislature. He fostered education both for public schools and for Montana Wesleyan University (now Rocky Mountain College). But we are probably most indebted to him for his support of the Historical Society.

Late in his life and again shortly after his death, his fellow

The Historical Society's office was moved to the capitol in 1902.

citizens showed their appreciation for his truly remarkable life. In February 1905, the legislature created Sanders County, just a few months before his death on July 17, 1905. After his death, fellow pioneer A.M. Holter headed up a Wilbur F. Sanders Memorial Association to solicit money for creation of a statue for the capitol. Assisted by a $5,000 appropriation from the legislature in 1911, the group was able to proceed with the creation of a statue finished in October 1912. Sanders' friends placed the statue in the capitol rotunda and unveiled it September 24, 1913. Governor Sam Stewart accepted it on behalf of the state. Later, public authorities moved the statue from the rotunda to the head of the grand staircase. More recently, Sanders' spot has given way to a larger-than-life statue of Jeannette Rankin, and Sanders has been relegated to a pigeon roost in the capitol's south side parking lot.

When the Montana Historical Society reorganized as a state agency in the 1890s, the board of trustees had to find a new librarian, a position that covered administration of all the Society's activities. In 1898, the board appointed Laura Spencer Howey.

Howey was born of old colonial stock in Cadiz, Ohio. After high school in her home town, she attended Beaver College in Beaver Falls, Pennsylvania, an early and prominent college for women. After college she studied library methods with Melville Dewey in Albany, New York. She also studied at the University of Wisconsin at Madison. After her arrival in Montana in 1879, she became very active in civic affairs. She served as secretary of the State Board of Charities, trustee of Helena's city library, state president of the WCTU, chair of the Board of Lady Managers for the Chicago World's Fair in 1893, and leader of the women's campaign on behalf of Helena as the state capital.

Not surprisingly, Howey proved to be a very capable librarian who catalogued the society's holdings, wrung appropriations from the state legislature, and secured new quarters in the capitol, all the while plugging for a new building. Unfortunately, she was the victim of an opinion by Attorney General Albert Galen that cut short her career.

Governor Joseph K. Toole had appointed several women as notaries public when someone called his attention to the fact that only qualified electors could hold public office. Galen's opinion said that the position of librarian was a public office and Mrs. Howey, by virtue of her womanhood, could not be an elector and therefore could not hold public office. Because Howey had made numerous friends through her library work and civic activities, Galen's opinion was widely unpopular, as reflected by the press. For example, the Stockgrowers *Journal,* a paper adamantly opposed to woman suffrage, said that if anything could get the paper to change its mind on this subject it would be Galen's opinion.

The person who bridged the gap between the firing of Mrs. Howey and the reorganization of the society in 1949 was Anne McDonnell. Her tenure as assistant librarian from 1923 to 1953 spanned that of several old-boy appointments as librarian. A Minnesotan, Anne came to Montana as a young girl. She worked for a time in the Butte Public Library and attended the Normal College at Dillon. She taught in various schools, including one near Lewistown where she met her husband-to-be. After a brief and unsatisfactory marriage, she came to Helena as assistant librarian, a position she held for the next thirty years. In addition to carrying on Howey's work of classifying materials for the library, she edited volume ten of the *Contributions* of the Historical Society. After *Montana: The Magazine of Western History* was established, she contributed numerous reviews and articles to the early issues.

Mrs. McDonnell was a truly remarkable person who carried around in her head a great deal of library information and historical facts. Joseph Kinsey Howard, in the acknowledgments in his famous book, *Montana High, Wide and Handsome,* said that "no one who writes, or even reads, Montana history can adequately tell what he owes to Mrs. Anne McDonnell." K. Ross Toole, who was briefly her boss, said that no living person "knows more about Montana's history." After her retirement because of failing eyesight, Toole added that, "She was the Historical Society."

In 1949, the legislature revealed a new enthusiasm for Montana history. It passed a complete recodification of the laws pertaining to the society and passed an appropriation for a new Veterans and Pioneers Memorial Building. In keeping with the new appreciation of local history, the board set about looking for a new director, as the administrative head of the new organization was now styled. The board's choice proved to be a most fortunate one who deserves credit for the creation of the Historical Society as we know it today.

K. Ross Toole, appointed director in 1951, was a fourth-generation Montanan on both sides of his family. A World War II veteran, he pursued his education briefly after his return from the war at Georgetown University and then at the University of Montana Law School. In the process he discovered that his first love was western history. With B.A. and M.A degrees under his arm from the University of Montana where he studied under Paul Phillips, he went to UCLA to study under John W. Caughey. Despite the fact that he had not finished the dissertation for the Ph.D. when he applied for the directorship, the thirty-year-old graduate student found enthusiastic supporters among the trustees, especially board president Norman Winestine and Montana State College history professor Merrill G. Burlingame.

As a scholar, Toole initially saw the library and archives as the society's principal program, but as director he had to assume responsibility for development of the institution on a broad front. For example, knowing little about museums, he turned to the Smithsonian Institution for help. That agency lent him one of its best western history personnel, John Ewers, who in a lifetime of study acquired national recognition for his knowledge and expertise in western museums. He also became a life-long friend of the Historical Society. In a short time, with Ewers' help, dioramas and displays began to appear on the building's walls.

In developing the directorship into a many-faceted position, Toole accepted personal responsibility for outreach. He talked to many service clubs and other organizations on the importance of local history. He frequently expounded on one of his favorite quotes from philosopher George Santayana, that those who do not remember their history are destined to repeat it.

Despite his varied responsibilities as director, Toole managed to finish his Ph.D., edit with Merrill Burlingame a two-volume history of Montana, and publish his first book, *Montana: An Uncommon Land* (1959), which received an Award of Merit from the Association of State and Local History and established Toole as the state's premier historian.

In 1958, with many achievements behind him, Toole resigned his directorship over the bitterness that surrounded the dismissal of Carl McFarland as president of the University of Montana. Toole accepted appointment as director of the Museum of the City of New York. After several years in an urban environment, Toole was lured back to the West in 1960 as director of museums for the state of New Mexico.

In 1963, Toole returned to Montana to run a ranch near Red Lodge. In 1965, he accepted appointment as Hammond Professor of Western History at the University of Montana, where he taught until his untimely death in 1981. In this position Toole directed numerous theses and dissertations that opened whole new areas of Montana history. Many of these student writings utilized the holdings of the Historical Society that Toole had developed.

Toole was probably the most popular lecturer in the history of the university. Attendance at his lectures often crowded out students officially enrolled in his course "Montana and the West." During his last year of teaching, he lectured to some 1,700 students. Toole's legacy as historian and writer is enormous, but probably his most lasting one will be the Historical Society.

Since his directorship, a few able directors and especially a professional staff of energetic and dedicated workers have developed a broad offering of programs for the public, some of which Toole established or had in mind. Professional historians, genealogists and local history buffs rely heavily on the library and its archival holdings of newspapers, state and territorial documents, books, pamphlets, regional periodicals and a large collection of photographs. The museum collects, preserves and displays fine art and artifacts. The art features the Mackay Collection of Charles M. Russell that Toole was largely responsible for securing. Other art collections generally reflect the tradition of western art. An exception is the highly valued and internationally known Poindexter Collection of Modern Art. The society's most recently established program is Historic Preservation, which assists individuals and groups who are seeking to preserve architectural and archeological resources.

Toole's vision of the society as the nucleus of a state scholarly press remains largely unfulfilled. His establishment of *Montana: The Magazine of Western History* is, in itself, a monument. The quarterly continues to have the largest circulation of any state journal in the country and it continues to achieve Toole's goal of a scholarly sound but attractively designed publication that appeals to the general reader as well as the professional. In addition to the magazine, the society has expanded its publication of books of local interest. Many people are aware of the press through its release of the acclaimed collection of literature, *The Last Best Place.*

While the society continues to get most of its support from legislative appropriations, it still depends on "soft money" from memberships, gifts and grants in order to maintain its full complement of programs. As measured by magazine subscriptions that confer society membership, Lewis and Clark County and the state as a whole are shamefully remiss in the support they give this invaluable institution. Only 4 percent of its membership comes from Lewis and Clark County and about 36 percent from the state as a whole. Thus more than 60 percent of its support comes from outside Montana. It appears that outsiders are more appreciative of this institution than Montana residents and are more willing and interested in lending the society their support.

ONE OF HELENA'S FIRST LADIES

BY HARRIETT C. MELOY

Meet Lizzie Fisk! A Helenan from 1867 to 1902, she was the wife of the mining camp's first newspaper editor, Robert Fisk. Strong and positive, independent and decisive, she emulated many women who traveled west in the early 1800s. She earned an exceptional place in our history because of the numerous letters she wrote to her Connecticut home from 1867 to 1893, which reveal a social history of Helena that does not appear in any other source.

Lizzie's story began in February 1846, at East Haddam, a small community along the Connecticut River. Her father was a farmer and a pastor. Her Methodist and Republican parents reared their daughters, Elizabeth and Fannie, conservatively. Lizzie completed her education in 1863 and became a teacher. Volunteers in the Civil War effort and members of the Vernon (Connecticut) Patriotic Society, the sisters sewed piecework quilts for the soldiers. Within one of the folded quilts, Lizzie placed a note giving her name and address. Captain Robert Emmett Fisk, a New York Volunteer in the 132nd Infantry, found the note and replied thanking the writer and asking her to write back. Thus began a correspondence between Elizabeth and Robert that lasted until the end of the war in 1865. That same year Robert traveled to Vernon to pay Elizabeth a visit, which culminated in their engagement.

Robert, however, did not have the pleasure of remaining near his betrothed, for he had made plans to join his brother in Minnesota for an expedition to the Montana gold fields. The expedition failed in 1865, but in 1866 Robert and James Fisk reached Helena, where they established a newspaper with the help of fellow Republicans. Robert served as the *Herald's* editor and acquired a business interest in the newspaper.

In 1867, he returned to Vernon and married Lizzie. Immediately the couple journeyed west. Their long Missouri River voyage motivated the homesick bride to begin correspondence with her Connecticut family. Describing life on a Missouri River boat, Lizzie wrote the first of 610 letters that comprise the day-by-day account of her sojourn in Montana from 1867 to the Silver Panic of 1893. Countless pioneer women chose diaries and journals to chronicle their experiences. But letters, different from diary tidbits and meditative journal accounts, appeared to be the more satisfying vehicle for women to tell their stories and express their opinions, hopes, fears, and feelings to loved ones left behind.

Apparently, Lizzie took to Helena life quickly. In a July 31, 1867, letter she wrote, "My first impressions of Helena have been generally confirmed. I like the place very much; it's not like home but there is a wide field of usefulness here, and, entering upon the work earnestly and prayerfully one need never be lonely or disheartened...I like the place." At a later date Mr. Smith of the newspaper staff asked if she liked this country. She replied, "I do like it. I am perfectly happy and content here, no one comes here to stay longer than until their fortunes are made and the idea of building a comfortable house and making a pleasant home is not for a moment cherished by a majority of our citizens. I tell everyone I expect to stay."

Lizzie's predilection toward a "wide field of usefulness" was exercised almost immediately when she began working in the *Herald* office "bookbinding [Helena Business Directories]." At this work she "persevered," finding her "reward in looking at the piles of pamphlets and the amount of money they represent to the *[Helena Herald]* office." But in her next letter she wondered, "Shall I selfishly address myself to money-getting and ignore the claims of society upon me, or shall my influence be used to bring about a better state of things?"

Before responding to the wider claims of her community, though, Lizzie knew that she must establish a home. When a close neighbor decided to leave Helena, Lizzie persuaded her husband to buy the house next door—and none too soon. For earlier than expected the Fisks were to become parents. (Even though Lizzie reported to her mother in June (1868) that she was "the only bride of last year who had not done her duty shall I say toward increasing the population of Helena...I never did like to be like everyone else.")

Lizzie Fisk.

While anticipating the birth of their first child, the Fisks decided that Lizzie should accompany Robert on one of his frequent trips east to be away for about a year and a half. Robert traveled to the nation's capital for political purposes and to New York to obtain newspaper advertising and supplies. Meanwhile, Lizzie visited her family in Vernon, where on May 29, 1869, Grace Chester Fisk was born. Several months after the baby's birth, the threesome returned to Helena. Lizzie was shocked to note the changes that had taken place during their absence. In April 1868, a fire had destroyed Helena's business district, followed two months later a by a more devastating fire.

Two years later, in October 1871, the Fisks' worst fears were realized when "we were awakened by the furious ringing of the door bell and the fearful news that the *Herald* office was on fire. So it proved, and we had to stand calmly by and see the labor and accumulations of five toilsome years swept away in an hour." In 1872, Lizzie reported another terrible fire, but this one spared the *Herald* office.

The *Herald* prospered, causing Robert to spend more and more time traveling. Lizzie enjoyed her new independent role. She reported to her mother that she liked an existence quite apart from the family. "I did not think it possible when Rob left this time that I could be so happy without him...but I have learned, if I knew it not before that one can be happy independent of externals..."

Despite her husband's rather frequent travels, Robert and Lizzie had six children between 1869 and 1882. Lizzie was a conscientious mother. Heavy demands on Lizzie, not only by her own brood but also from her husband's numerous relatives, took their toll of time and strength. Nevertheless, Lizzie constantly yearned to confirm her usefulness to the community. She wrote to her mother, "An earnest woman wields a vast amount of influence in this community as in any other, but it seems here to be so much more needed and widely felt."

Given Lizzie's conservative and religious upbringing, she was particularly concerned about the community's religious well-being. In a letter she wrote: "Let me tell you how the wants and needs of ten thousand people are cared for." She writes of a Rev. Baxter of the first church established in Helena—a Methodist church. The pastor has 12 to 14 children, "the care of which clipped the wings of his mental and spiritual powers." She then describes Rev. Comfort, a new pastor "who while a good man is very illiterate and his remarks are not always in good taste. People receive him kindly and his congregations are larger than of old..." But "Where," she asks, "are the thousands who should assemble on Sunday and worship God? Where are Helena people on the Sabbath?"

Lizzie describes plans for a fair to be given by the Methodist church. When she heard there was to be dancing she lost interest. "I told the ladies that to me it was a very mean way of doing business and at length my patience gave out and I advised them to rent a dance hall on Main Street, employ hurdy girls and open a faro bank." Ironically, her name was entered—much to her chagrin—in a popularity contest held during the week of the fair. When the polls closed Saturday night, she was "three hundred votes ahead of all competition." She credited success to her opposition to church dancing!

In July of 1877, a new minister was called to the Methodist church, but Lizzie was not charmed with him. "Occasionally he preaches a good sermon, but his voice is bad and his manner and gestures more forcible than graceful...Our congregation and Sunday School are very small this summer." Perhaps even Lizzie slacked in her attendance, for church and religion almost disappeared from her letters during the next few years.

Besides religion, Lizzie was concerned about education in Helena. Her appreciation of the schools and teachers blew hot and cold. For instance, in February 1879 she wrote: "Gracie is blessed with a most excellent teacher, Mrs. D.M. Darnold. She teaches because she loves to work, though she has a husband both able and willing to take care of her. She is a lady ever and always and I feel assured that Grace is not learning from her that which she must unlearn at home. But the children with whom she comes in contact are with few exceptions, ignorant, vulgar, uncouth, and 'full of all subtlety and mischief'."

About son Robbie's teacher, Lizzie wrote, "She has one idea ever uppermost, which is that she is getting on in years and is still unmarried. She has 'set her cap' for every eligible bachelor in the place, thus far to no avail."

In February of 1880, Lizzie informs her mother, "I do not intend sending Grace and Robbie to school again this winter…I have long been dissatisfied with the school. Mr. Howie, the principal, is an excellent Christian man. But Gracie's teacher, the Miss Helen Clark[e] is a half-breed Indian, the daughter of Malcolm Clark[e] , who you perhaps remember, was killed by the Indians nearly eleven years ago. Miss C. was educated in a convent and is avowedly a Catholic but she has no faith in God or man. She hates the school, hates her work. While I am sorry for her, she is not the one I would choose for the education of my children." She ended her letter by saying, "I would like to see a half-dozen Yankee teachers filling positions in our schools, young ladies educated thoroughly for their work."

When Lizzie took her children out of the public schools, as she did from time to time, she taught them herself. Yet after a few months the children returned to Helena schools, allowing Lizzie her "wider field of usefulness." She joined the Women's Christian Temperance Union in the hope of affecting change in another disturbing aspect of life in her community—alcohol consumption.

In one of Lizzie's letters, she describes the plight of a man whom Robert had left in charge of the *Herald* while he was in the East: "…If I needed any reminder of the peril of touching one drop of ardent spirits the lesson has been brought home to me…during the three last weeks. I cannot understand how any man can be as lost to every principle of manhood as to seek in intoxication relief from sorrow."

In April 1890 Rob's brother, Van Fisk, died of alcoholism. A letter in January laments: "Uncle Van...has been drinking hard for more than a year...It was a relief to everyone when his sufferings were over."

After Tommy Cruse's 1888 wedding, Lizzie wrote, "I never felt the need of temperance work so greatly as since the Cruse wedding. Just think of the boys who have grown up in our midst who were that day sent home to their mothers intoxicated. Think of the men who made beasts of themselves because the wine was free."

Other challenges sprang up as Helena continued to grow. Lizzie did not fail to notice and to act. She wrote in 1887: "Our 'poor committee' has been kept busy. There are many cases of weakness and destitution. Men out of work... Mothers deserted, or robbed of the husband and father by death ...Girls coming here in search of work who are friendless and who need some place where they can stay." Lizzie and her women friends worked to acquire a home for indigent families and girls who came to Helena in search of work.

Lizzie's religious fervor and love for mankind, unfortunately, was not extended to Montana's Indians. In a letter to her mother relating a description of the Big Hole Battle, she wrote: "War is so cruel; and it does seem that to be shot down by savages is almost throwing one's life away. Any one of those brave men who was sacrificed in the Big Hole battle was worth more than all the Indians in the country and yet every year thousands of just such men are slain and our 'Indian Policy' remains not unchanged but ever changing for the worse. The only comfort, and only safety, of the extreme West lies in total extermination of the savage...."

Lizzie's ambition to exert "a wide field of usefulness" in the place where she had lived most of her adult life was being realized. Moreover, her accomplishment was nearly coming to fruition through the bonding of women who shared her dream, willing to work beside her to make the dream come true. A growing network of other similarly committed women was the final key to success in Lizzie's pursuit of a better life for Helena. Lizzie's preserved correspondence defined the progress of this pursuit.

HELEN CLARKE

BY HARRIETT C. MELOY

Only a very few women's biographies appear in the half-dozen "mug" books on the shelves of the Montana Historical Society library. One of the unsung heroines of Montana history, a fascinating woman by the name of Helen Piotopowaka Clarke, became a scholar and educator, as well as an artist and actress. She possessed a knack for politics that led her to seek the office of Lewis and Clark County superintendent of schools in 1882. She ran on the Republican ticket and won handily, being also endorsed by the county Democrats. Later she served the U.S. government in parceling lands to Indian people after the Indian Allotment Act of 1887 passed.

Born at the mouth of the Judith River (now Fergus County), on October 11, 1848, Helen was the daughter of a Piegan princess and a former West Point cadet. Helen's father, Malcolm Clarke, the son of Lieutenant Nathan Clarke of the 5th Infantry Regiment, entered West Point at the age of 17. A promising student and an unusually eloquent talker, he won the approval of officers and peers alike. But, unfortunately, according to his sister Charlotte, his exaggerated "sense of honor" and a fierce temper led him into trouble. When one of his company accused him of making a false report about a dereliction of duty, young Malcolm flogged the student and thus set himself up for a court-martial. Clarke left the academy, and with the help of Captain John Culbertson, his father's lifelong friend, he obtained an appointment to the American Fur Company on the Upper Missouri in 1841. Trading successfully among the Indians, he won their confidence and married Cothcocona, daughter of a Blackfeet tribal chief.

Malcolm Clarke persisted in fur trading and the pursuit of

an itinerant life until 1864 when he moved his trading post to the Prickly Pear Valley, about twenty miles north of Helena. There he began raising cattle and putting down roots for his wife and children—Helen, Isabel, Horace and Nathan. Besides forsaking his traditional nomadic lifestyle, he pledged to send his children east to live with relatives where they could obtain the best education possible. Malcolm arranged with his sister, Charlotte Ouisconsin Clarke Van Cleve, to take the children into her Minneapolis home and oversee their education.

According to her father's wishes, Helen became well schooled in Minneapolis and continued more advanced education in Cincinnati with another aunt, where she acquired a taste for fine literature, art and drama. While touring with a company from a New York drama school, she became an accomplished actress and attained recognition in the capitals of Europe for her interpretation of Lady Macbeth. Both the German Kaiser and the Queen of the Netherlands wrote letters of commendation about Helen's performances.

Successful though she was, Helen was not happy. Much later, a clue to her unhappiness and the longing for the land of her birth appears in a letter to a friend, Miss O'Neill. Helen wrote that "the cities with their 'madding crowds' have so little attraction that I can say with so much earnestness on leaving them 'goodbye proud world I am going home'."

When Helen returned to the Prickly Pear Valley in 1864, all was not well between the Blackfeet and white settlers. Trouble intensified over the next decade. In the aftermath of Governor Thomas Francis Meagher's ill-conceived 1867 "Indian wars," two Blackfeet youths were gunned down at Fort Benton for no apparent reason. One of the young men was the brother of Mountain Chief, a prominent Blackfeet leader. The Piegans (one branch of the Blackfeet) and their friends the Sioux went on raiding parties, stealing horses and killing livestock in retaliation for the slaying.

On a sunny August morning in 1869, a party of Pikani (another Blackfeet branch), led by a nephew of Cothcocona rode up to Malcolm Clarke's home, ostensibly searching for lost horses but actually intending to murder the Clarke family. When they left, Horace, Clarke's son, was injured and left for dead and Malcolm was fatally shot.

Although Mrs. Malcolm Clarke was at the family home at the time of the tragedy, it appears fairly certain she could do nothing to stop the killing. Little is known about Helen's mother; the only reference in the literature of the day is a Great Falls *Leader* obituary dated June 1895 that reported

Helen Clarke.

the death of Mrs. Malcolm Clarke at her son Horace's home at Midvale (Glacier Park). In his memoir, written in 1924, Horace commented that the shock of his father's death and his own near demise drove his mother to madness from which she never recovered.

After the incident, Helen Clarke left her father's home and the family she loved, to teach school in Fort Benton. She then responded to an invitation by Wilbur F. Sanders to come to Helena "to take charge of a classroom." A protege of the Sanders family, she became popular in the territorial capital almost immediately. Highly educated and winsome, she taught in Helena's schools and also performed as an actress whenever invited to do so. White Sulphur Springs was the site of one of her performances in 1880, where she receive abundant accolades for her portrayal of Lady Macbeth.

Helen's success as a teacher well qualified her to seek the

office of county superintendent of schools for Lewis and Clark County in 1882. She became the first woman to hold an elective office in the Territory of Montana. A perfectionist always, she was disappointed in 1883 that her June institutes for teacher training were not well attended. But, according to the 1883 annual report of the Superintendent of Public Instruction, blame for the small attendance in "no degree attaches to the efficiency of Supt. Miss Helen Clarke."

Helen served the county public schools from 1882 to 1888, but she desired a wider range of action than the school superintendency offered. Her financial resources were limited, as was the vocational potential for women in the late 1800s. Since she was an unusually attractive woman, and popular, some Helena friends wondered why she did not marry. In a *Grass Range Review* article Helen explained that "she never married because of her part Indian blood. She felt that she might not be regarded as an equal in a match with a white man, and she did not care to enter into any arrangement where there might be the least idea of inequality." Evidently she did not consider marrying a man of her mother's race.

In 1887 the Indian Allotment Act passed, and Helen Clarke was invited to act as interpreter and mediator for the Blackfeet during their application for allotment land. In this position she was so effective that her ability came to the attention of the Office of Indian Affairs which appointed her, in 1891, to a position in Oklahoma to make allotments to the Ponca, Oto, Pawnee, and Tonkawa Indians of that state. She was credited as being one of the few women who assisted in managing the federal Indian program.

When allotment work subsided throughout the country, Helen went to San Francisco where she had friends who helped her to find work. However, in 1902 a long-pending claim related to her father's death was resolved in the federal court of claims. She was awarded $2,490. With this money she joined her brother in the cattle business in Midvale. She lived there until her death on March 7, 1923, in her home nestled amidst the grandeur of peaks and valleys of Blackfeet country that later became Glacier National Park.

Hats Trim a Helena Family Tree

By Ellen Baumler

Most families have a few stories about their forebears tucked away, perhaps remembered only by Grandma or Grandpa, that are occasionally told around the family dinner table. Nothing should be more cherished than stories like these, for they can transport us to another time and acquaint us with those whom we never knew. The Morris-Silverman family is rich in such family lore. Several charming stories in particular, now enjoyed by fourth and fifth generations of that family, revolve around a Victorian-era institution: ladies' hats.

Essie Morris and Moz J. Silverman were married on June 28, 1905. Two years before on that same June day, a group of six young people had climbed to the top of Mount. Helena "for the novelty and adventure of the thing," as the newspaper's society editor later reported. The ladies present had promised their mothers that the young men of the party would build a bonfire on the top of the mountain to signal a successful ascent.

As the times dictated, Essie's proper attire for this outing included a large picture hat. Upon reaching the summit, she tossed the hat aside and a few moments later realized that it had landed in the fire. The beautiful hat was a total loss. When Essie later told the story, she said that Moz had seized the opportunity to turn catastrophe into a proposal saying, "Miss Essie, I'd like nothing better than the privilege of buying your hats for the rest of your life!" Essie said yes, and the reporter summed it up: "Thus another romance is added to the long list for which Mt. Helena is responsible." And all this because of a pretty picture hat! The wedding took place in the Morris family's residence at 403 North Ewing. Essie wore her mother's wedding veil.

Essie's mother, Emma Amson Morris, had been married under different circumstances in very different times during the 1870s. Helena was not much more than a gold camp. Permanency was just taking root in this remote and isolated town,

SYDNEY SILVERMAN LINDAUER

Essie Morris Silverman around the time of her marriage, in 1905.

but at the same time an astonishing array of material accoutrements were being introduced to the "civilized" world. Domestic electric lighting, the horseless carriage, the phonograph and the bicycle all made their debuts in the 1870s. Even here in Helena, the French Second Empire influenced local architecture and Paris dictated the latest fashion trends.

The changes that occurred during the last decades of the nineteenth century—culminating in Essie's turn-of-the-century picture hat—were every bit as innovative as those "new-fan-gled" inventions. It was this age that put away the hoop skirt in favor of the bustle. Publications like *Godey's Lady's Book* and *Harper's* brought these fashions to American women even on the western frontier. The well-dressed woman of the 1870s "...fastened to her head pounds of hair shorn from the heads of God knows whom and to her rear attached an avalanche of drapery upon the hillock of a bustle." This was the time period when Lily Langtry represented the epitome of American beauty. "Real men" disdained the English fashion of carrying an unneeded cane and made fun of contemporaries who wore a monocle. Men who had the nerve to follow these fads were labeled "dudes" (indeed!) and "la-de-dah boys."

Such were the fashion trends when Helena merchant Moses Morris set out on the stage bound for the nearest Union Pacific station at Corinne, Utah. After a journey of five days and nights, he boarded the train east to St. Louis where, on April 14, 1878, Moses married eighteen-year-old Emma Amson. Like so many plucky women of that era, Emma was prepared to make her home on the frontier. She had neatly folded and packed her trousseau—"one dozen of everything, all monogrammed by hand"—in trunks and boxes which would be sent to her new home in far away Montana Territory. The newlyweds traveled up the Missouri on the steamer *Western* and arrived at Fort Benton on June 20. They continued overland to Helena by stage.

Once settled, Emma waited anxiously for all her "pretties" to arrive. Finally on July 25, the long-awaited boxes and trunks were unloaded in front of the Morris brothers' store on North Main Street. But alas, before the precious items could be brought to the house, a most peculiar storm sent a torrent of water rushing along Helena's streets. The *Daily Independent* reported that a "canoe could have been floated" on the major thoroughfares. "Dry goods boxes, doors, chicken coops, clothing, kitchen utensils, fragments of gates etc." rushed along in the flood. Among the casualties of this disaster were the carefully-packed trunks and boxes of Emma Morris' trousseau, which had "tumbled end over end, all the way to the open prairie...and burst wide open."

The memory of this rude welcome to Helena did not, apparently, dampen Emma's indomitable spirit, but it must have pained her mightily to see her once-beautiful linens "decorating the sagebrush." It was, therefore, doubly exciting when Moses proposed a trip home to St. Louis a few years later. Suddenly, Emma later confessed, she began to feel "most dowdy." A trip to the milliner quelled her fears when the hatmaker promised to make a hat that would prove Helena a cosmopolitan town quite in touch with the very latest styles.

Since the onset of the 1880s, hats had become increasingly complicated, adorned with all manner of feathers, plumes, birds, leaves, grasses, oats, "dandelion clocks," birds' nests and other natural—and not so natural—wonders. The milliners price was exorbitant but Emma was delighted with her stylish concoction: "...it was trimmed with flowers, grasses, bits of fur and a feather or two—well," as Emma told the story, "it would have been easier to name what wasn't on that hat...."

Emma was a tiny woman and the fancy hat was rather large and hard to manage. Several days had passed as the train rolled along toward St. Louis. Emma and a few other passengers stood on the rear platform admiring the view when a sudden gust of wind caught the hat and sent it cart-wheeling across the landscape. Emma wept over the loss of her fabulous hat.

As the train reached its destination, Emma's stylish St. Louis friends were waiting at the station. "I took one long look at them," as she later told it, "and murmured to myself that maybe it was a good thing the wind took that hat."

Certainly there was sorrow for Emma and Moses, who lost three sons during the 1880s, and for Moz Silverman when Essie died prematurely in 1929. But Emma's and Essie's stories are remembered still by their children, grandchildren and great-grandchildren.

Marvelous stories like these from another time serve to remind us that our experiences today, no matter how trivial, will become history tomorrow. May we savor life's little joys and remember to share them with our children!

Many thanks to my friend, Sydney Silverman Lindauer (Essie's daughter and Emma's granddaughter), who so graciously and enthusiastically shared her family album.

Depression Gangsters— Helena Style

By Dave Walter

At noon on June 18, 1929, two masked men robbed the Ronan State Bank and escaped in a green Hudson touring car. They stole $3,000—half of which pack rats ate before it could be spent. They injured two bank employees, although both recovered. Authorities fairly quickly captured the robbers, as well as their drivers. The perpetrators of this daring Ronan robbery were incarcerated at the Deer Lodge prison by November.

This would seem to be a simple event proving that "crime does not pay." Instead, it exposes a more complicated story of violent felons, Depression style—featuring a Helena-based gang of criminals.

By 1929 Montana's long agricultural depression had moved into the towns. On the national scene, Herbert Hoover had just been elected President. Montana prohibition was eleven years old; national Prohibition was ten, and still four years short of repeal. The 1920s had spawned jazz, a new kind of cynicism about work, the weakening of long-held taboos, "talkies," Charles Lindbergh's transatlantic flight, and a collective self-indulgence. By 1929 one in every five Americans owned an automobile, as autos had evolved from oddities to necessities to status symbols.

Historians either credit Prohibition with creating a decade of concerted hypocrisy, or they treat it as the by-product of a new national naughtiness. Regardless, Prohibition produced gangsters. And, in their romanticized lawlessness, gangsters provided liquor and other illegal pleasures. Then, on "Black Tuesday" (October 29, 1929), the stock market crashed. Fi-

Easton Boone.

nally the whole nation knew what Montana farmers and ranchers had been saying throughout the 1920s: "Tough times are *here!*" The robbery of the Ronan State Bank and its related crimes fit neatly into the final months of the 1920s.

The four men who robbed the Ronan bank vanished into thin air by cleverly relying on two escape cars, two drivers, and a prearranged meeting place in the woods near Pablo. While frantic authorities roared up and down gravel-covered U.S. 93, the thieves calmly drove south to Missoula in a second touring car.

The Burns Detective Agency, hired by the American Banking Association, sent its representative from Spokane, Washington, immediately. But only when a local rancher spotted the abandoned green Hudson in the woods near Pablo could authorities proceed. At the site of the auto, Lake County Sheriff W.H. Needham found tire tracks from the getaway car, the remains of a campfire, a burned cap with the name "Ganny" inside it, a matchbook, pieces of hotel stationery with a handwritten address on it, a pair of coveralls, and a dropped roll of bills.

From these clues, Needham linked the matchbook to The Mint—a Helena saloon converted to a cigar store by Prohibition. He also traced the stationery to the Placer Hotel in Helena. He discovered "Ganny" to be Ganny Boone, whose family lived at the Helena address scrawled on the stationery. Ganny proved a reliable character, but he had a ne'er-do-well brother, Easton, whose arrest record for fighting and Prohibition violations made him a suspect.

By June 20, the *Ronan Pioneer* asserted: "The robbery is without doubt the work of an expert gang and was carefully planned out….No effort is being spared to bring about the gang's capture."

Once linked with Lewis and Clark County Sheriff Clyde Burgess, Sheriff Needham traveled to Helena to arrest Easton

Boone on June 23. By June 27, Boone had been bound over to district court in Polson. Boone neither confessed to the crime nor implicated anyone.

Martin Jensen.

Speculative newspaper accounts of "Montana's expert gang of bank robbers" provided high melodrama week after week. By September, Needham and law-enforcement officers in Helena, Anaconda, Great Falls, Boulder, Missoula, and St. Ignatius could prove that the Ronan bank job had been committed by four men—part of a seven-member gang.

Easton Boone and Martin Jensen were the two masked men who had robbed the Ronan State Bank on June 18. Martin Ernst and Joe Brennan served as their drivers.

These four men were young—in their twenties—with shady reputations and small-time records. The gang also included Tom Martin, Floyd Grote, and Robert Bowers. Martin was an older, savvy criminal who sported a long record of serious crimes throughout the West. Joe Brennan's wife and a Helena floozy named Bobby Kelly (see following article) often accompanied these characters.

The story of how Montana lawmen investigated and captured the bank-robbery gang enlivened the front pages of Montana newspapers throughout the summer of 1929. Each development in this dramatic soap-opera left the statewide audience begging for the next episode. The saga includes several key incidents.

On July 14, 1929, unidentified robbers hit the Green Mill (Lantern) Dance Hall near Great Falls and took about $1,000. Authorities found no immediate link between this holdup and the Ronan bank job.

Two days later, on July 16, Sheriff Needham captured the second Ronan robber, Martin Ernst, in Anaconda. Officers had tracked Ernst's big Buick from Ronan to Lincoln to Helena and finally to Anaconda. Montana newspapers surmised that lawmen now knew the other members of the gang and that the search focused on Helena.

On July 23 "thugs" brandishing automatic pistols robbed and severely beat the ticket agent and a waiting passenger at the elegant Great Northern Depot on Helena's Neill Avenue (the current site of the Federal Reserve Bank, across from Hill Park). Witnesses watched the robbers leave the depot, climb into their "machine," and race west out of town. The informants could not agree, however, on a description of the men or of the automobile.

That night, on the Helena-Great Falls road (U.S. 91), highwaymen in two cars (a coupe and a sedan) stopped, beat, and robbed three Butte travelers. A bit later, several thieves held up a filling station in Wolf Creek. The coupe turned out to be a Studebaker stolen from the Chevalier Ranch north of Helena.

By the next afternoon—based on automobile and license-tag identifications and on an anonymous telephone call—sheriffs and their deputies from Cascade County and from Lewis and Clark County surrounded and ambushed a shack on the Missouri River southwest of Great Falls. With a volley of shots, they flushed from the cabin two men who surrendered—Martin Jensen and Robert Bowers. Two other occupants, Tom Martin and Floyd Grote, ran into the trees and escaped. Martin and Grote had deliberately sacrificed the youngest members of the gang for their own freedom.

With the capture of Jensen and Bowers, officers received a break in the case: Jensen talked! He admitted his role in the Green Mill dance-hall robbery and in the Great Northern depot holdup. In addition, he fingered Tom Martin and Floyd Grote as "the brains of the operation."

Just over a week later, Jensen and Bowers pled guilty to the Green Mill dance-hall felony, and each received a sentence of twenty years in the Montana State Prison. Neither young man confessed to more than standing guard during the Great Northern depot heist. Both did admit, however, that Martin had lured them into similar ventures with the promise of "easy money." Newspapers revealed that the "green getaway machine" used was a green Marquette sedan stolen in Sandpoint, Idaho.

Suddenly the scene of Montana's summer-long melodrama shifted back to western Montana. On August 19 Easton Boone's trial began in Polson, where Helena attorney Lester Loble defended him. Martin Ernst's trial would follow immediately in the Lake County seat.

Then shortly after midnight on August 20—just down the road from Polson in St. Ignatius—three bandits awoke Mission State Bank cashier A.P. Morse and his family in their beds. Two criminals drove Morse to his bank at gunpoint and demanded that he open the safe. But the Mission State Bank recently had installed an electric timer on its vault. So the thwarted trio forced Morse to carry the bank's loose coins to his home, gathered up his wife and two small children, and pushed them into getaway cars.

The thieves and their hostages drove south in the Morses' brand new Nash and in a green Oakland coach. On Evaro Hill, when the Nash ran out of gasoline, the bandits punctured its tires, abandoned the family, and headed toward Missoula in the Oakland. Morse reported that only one gunman had worn a mask and that another (apparently the leader) was talkative and drunk—sipping moonshine during much of the escapade.

Joe Brennan.

Two days later, Lewis and Clark County Sheriff Burgess began receiving reports that the Oakland coach had been seen in Helena, then in Boulder, and then in Meaderville (adjacent to Butte). A clerk in a Boulder soft-drink parlor tentatively identified the suspects as Joe Brennan, Tom Martin, and another person, probably a woman.

Then, on the night of August 21, Butte businessman James Thomas pulled over on his way home from Anaconda to help what seemed to be a stranded woman motorist—"a woman dressed all in white." Two men quickly appeared from the shadows, bound and gagged Thomas, and stole his Hudson. Before departing they pushed the green Oakland coach used in the St. Ignatius robbery into the borrow pit and set it afire. The next day, the Montana Bankers Association called attention to its $2,000 reward to the person who could produce "any dead bank robbers."

The Boone trial in Polson ended in a hung jury, after the defendant produced family members and friends who placed him in several Helena locations on June 18. The prosecution mustered stronger evidence in the Ernst trial. The Lake County jury quickly convicted him, and he spent the night preparing his full confession.

On August 31, lawmen ambushed whiskey-runner Tom Flavin's cabin south of Helena, in Jefferson County. Armed with sawed-off shotguns and repeating rifles, officers surrounded the shack while Sheriff Burgess coasted his police car down the slope above the cabin and shined a spotlight directly inside. After a few warning shots, Joe Brennan's wife and Bobby Kelly appeared, dressed in coveralls, and surrendered. When no one else emerged, officers opened fire on the cabin. Tom Martin and Joe Brennan quickly shouted that they too would surrender.

Authorities never did locate Floyd Grote—either that autumn or later. In perfunctory ten-minute proceedings in Polson on September 10, Easton Boone and Joe Brennan pled guilty to the Ronan State Bank robbery. They entered the Montana State Prison on September 12, each with a fifteen-year sentence.

Bobby Kelly—"the woman in white"—confessed to nothing. In fact, during September she waffled: first she offered to "tell all" in exchange for immunity, and then she insisted on her innocence. Kelly was described (Helena *Montana Record-Herald,* September 6, 1929) as "...unusually attractive,...[although] her speech teems with the vernacular of the street....Mrs. Kelly continued to keep up her chic appearance when she appeared for her hearing at Anaconda clad in a Lindbergh helmet, black coat, sheer silk hose, and spike-heeled shoes."

In October, Kelly finally stood trial in Anaconda. She pled not guilty on all charges. Her attorney portrayed her as an innocent victim of circumstances, who was blinded by alcohol to the effects of her actions. Tom Martin testified in her defense that, in fact, he had kept her ignorant of all the plots. The jury acquitted "the woman in white."

Tom Martin, the real leader of the gang, was tried in Helena for the Great Northern depot robbery. Prosecutors relied heavily on the eyewitness testimony of the beaten railroad clerk. The jury deliberated only ten minutes before convicting Martin on November 7. Authorities immediately escorted him to the Deer Lodge prison to begin a fifty-year term.

A look at this brief episode of Helena history provides more than just lurid reading. It produces more than just a glimpse of Montana's low-budget version of the Al Capone hoodlums or the Bugsie Moran gang. The story truly reveals life in Montana during the late 1920s. For example, the only paved roads in the state were short stretches around Butte and Anaconda. So lawmen often used a combination of railroad and automobile travel to cover the state—and all auto travel was seasonal.

Also typical of the era, gang members brazenly drove stolen, flamboyant, touring-car "machines"—not Model-A Fords—in committing their crimes. And local lawmen welcomed trained-detective assistance from such companies as the Burns Detective Agency and the Great Northern Railway Company.

Justice in the 1920s also seems swift by current standards. The judicial system brought accused criminals to trial quickly, and a guilty verdict resulted in an immediate, stiff sentence and imprisonment. In the case of the seven Helena gang members, authorities concluded *all* legal action less than five months after the *beginning* of their crime spree!

What the 1929 story of the Helena gangsters best reveals is how susceptible the Montana public was to a continuing saga of outrageous crime—complete with fast cars, unnecessary violence, a mysterious "woman in white," and methodical, unrelenting lawmen. Montanans displayed a voracious appetite for every tidbit of this story fed to them by local newspapers. A parallel exists with the year-long O.J. Simpson trial and the grip it exerted on the American public via television. Fortunately for Montanans, Helena's 1929 gangsters experienced a much shorter run.

THE MYSTERIOUS MURDER
OF THE "WOMAN IN WHITE"

BY DAVE WALTER

Behind the thin veil that separates the known from the unknown in the Margaret (Bobby) Kelly murder case, there surges a score of shadowy figures, barely discernible, whose motives and doings would furnish the most skilled weaver of detective tales with a plot beyond the wildest dreams of his imagination.

These figures are silent as the tomb. They flit swiftly to and fro, and from their passings emanates a cold, menacing breath like that from some dismal morass. They are on the "inside" and, through mysterious sources of information, learn in advance what the next move will be. They have influences in high places; they pull strings, and puppets move to do their bidding. Their shadows fall like the chill of cold steel, and warm flesh trembles. But their identities are never revealed.

W. W. Casper,
Helena *Montana Record-Herald*, March 12, 1930

The story of the 1929 Ronan bank robbery (see preceding essay)—complete with flashy getaway cars, intuitive sleuthing, weak-charactered and easy-talking witnesses, and a classic log-cabin shootout—may not have ended that November with the conviction and imprisonment of gang leader Tom Martin. In what seems a sensational sequel, Margaret "Bobby" Kelly ("the woman in white") was shot to death in a Helena apartment on December 2, 1929.

Two months before her murder, Kelly had been acquitted of any complicity in the gang's activities. Bobby had portrayed

HELENA INDEPENDENT, MAR. 8, 1930 (JANCU), AND DEC. 5, 1929

Nick Jancu

Bobby
Kelly
(right)
and
Jean
Mills
(far
right)

herself then as Martin's drunken, unknowing captive—a woman simply used as a decoy. Somewhat surprisingly, she escaped any implication during the subsequent confessions and trials. Finally all of the confessed or convicted gang members had been hauled off to the state prison in Deer Lodge. Only Floyd Grote escaped authorities, possibly by fleeing to Canada.

Late on Monday evening, December 2, 1929—less than a month after Martin began his prison sentence—Bobby Kelly was found shot to death at 13½ South Main Street, in the upstairs of Helena's Novelty Block. Bobby's business partner, Jean Mills, remained barely conscious in the blood-soaked apartment. Shot twice in the face, Miss Mills' groans and thuds finally attracted help. She was so badly wounded that no one expected her to live. However, within twenty-four hours, Jean Mills was able to tell the first of her several contradictory stories. Within 10 days, authorities jailed a suspect. His trial began on March 6, 1930, and ended nine days later.

The Montana newspaper coverage of these shootings, and of the investigation and trial that followed, proved both intense and sensational. It illustrates Montanans' continued love-hate relationship with Depression-era gangland crime and with its high-living men and women. It reveals also the vagaries of criminal-investigation procedures and of the judicial system of the time. Montana history books will not linger long over either the murder of "the woman in white" or the crime spree that preceded it. But the two incidents remain riveting in their portrayal of a Montana society early in the Great Depression.

As Helena's *Montana Record-Herald* delicately noted during the trial of the murder suspect, Bobby Kelly and Jean Mills belonged to "the world's oldest profession." The *Record-Herald* described Bobby as "unusually attractive, about 25 years of age, 5-foot 4-inches in height, dark auburn hair and eyes, addicted to the argot of the underworld, but at one time a person of education and refinement." Jean was older, sported red hair and blue eyes, and was about 5-foot 6-inches tall. Since she survived the attack, local papers avoided the painful characterizations of Jean that they offered for Bobby.

On that evening of December 2, 1929, Helenans Charles Moreau and David Johns found the Novelty Block's upstairs apartment door locked and heard groans inside. After several attempts to talk to Mills or Kelly, the two men summoned Helena police. Sometime after 10 P.M., Police Sergeant Earl Brown, Patrolman Tony Hames, Moreau, and Johns pounded on the apartment door. Finally a bloody Jean Mills dragged herself to the door and unbolted it. The men found Bobby Kelly's body in her room, "clad in silk undergarments, stockings, and slippers."

At Miss Mills' request, the men carried her to her blood-stained bed. She told officers that she was cold and that her ear hurt. Her bloody, puffy face hid two bullet holes. The officers kept her in bed while looking over the crime scene. They then called Coroner David T. Berg, County Attorney G.W. Padbury, Jr., Helena Police Chief Joe Spurzem, and Lewis and Clark County Sheriff Claude L. Burgess. At about 11 P.M., the four police officers, the two local citizens, and the two county officials thoroughly searched the Novelty Block apartment. During this period, the only name that officers heard Miss Mills utter was "Frank." The authorities allowed no one else inside the apartment. They discovered that Bobby Kelly's watch had stopped at 6:15—the time thereafter assumed to mark her death.

After 11 P.M., authorities took Jean Mills to nearby St. Peter's Hospital and placed her under the care of Dr. B.C. Shearer. Using X-ray equipment, Dr. Shearer found the bullet holes and some bullet fragments in her skull. He indicated to the press that she was close to death. However, he also participated in interviews with Mills and granted assorted officers interviews with her! Trial testimony, for instance, revealed that Sheriff Burgess had sent Goldie Morris, proprietress of the

Montana Hotel in the Novelty Block, to the hospital at 4 A.M. on December 3. Burgess had instructed Morris to see what specifics Jean might tell her that she would tell no one else.

By Thursday evening, December 5, the *Record-Herald* carried news of the murder under a banner headline: GANG GUN SILENCES GIRL. This headline was based on Mills' statements to Dr. Shearer on the morning after the shooting. The press concluded that Bobby knew too much about the Helena gang's activities and had paid for her knowledge of the summer crime spree with her life. Some journalists further speculated that Bobby had hidden the Ronan-bank money herself, paying the robbers with personal checks.

Other journalists agreed that Bobby knew much about the gang, but believed that she never had taken a role in the Ronan affair. County Attorney Padbury thought it likely that the crime was related to gang activity, but said that he also was investigating jealousy as a motive. Sheriff Burgess concluded that Bobby was killed by a "degenerate with an insane desire to kill."

The papers then reported a series of contradictory statements delivered by Jean Mills: (1) that there were two assailants, one wearing a sheepskin coat; (2) that there was only one attacker; (3) that she knew neither assailant; (4) that one looked like "Nick," a friend of Bobby's, but was not Nick; (5) that the single assailant was Nick; (6) that she surely had wounded the murderer—for she was awakened by the sound of the shot that killed Kelly and had confronted and fired at the intruder.

Sheriff Burgess made repeated trips to the gory crime scene to gather the two women's possessions—since he was investigating robbery as a possible motive. For a couple days, the papers described mass confusion regarding the whereabouts of the women's jewelry and cash. But Burgess found no substantive robbery clues, and he did locate the jewelry and money that Jean Mills had identified.

Brief speculation surfaced that Bobby and Jean simply had quarreled. To this end, lawmen interviewed Mabel Stitt, the African-American maid, and Dollie Miller, the laundress—but both had left the apartment between 5 P.M. and 6 P.M. The "quarrel theory" quickly died.

A week after the shootings, a *Record-Herald* reporter (*not* lawmen) found bullet holes, fingerprints, and blood smears that corroborated Jean Mills' description of her movements and the likelihood that she had shot at least one assailant. Both Helena papers then ran a blizzard of leads and speculations: of a maroon car, seen in front of the Novelty Block, that sped off on the East Helena Road; of bloody clothes taken by taxi to the Northern Pacific Depot and shipped out; of a Spanish .38-caliber pistol purchased at a secondhand store in Helena that week; of a picture of Larry Brennan (the brother of Ronan bank robber Joe Brennan) found on Kelly's bureau; of a bottle of moonshine sitting on Bobby's chiffonier (chest of drawers).

Officials conducted no inquest into Bobby Kelly's death. Her funeral was held on December 7, after her divorced parents had arrived in Helena from two separate locations. Kelly's mother fainted when escorted to the crime scene. The papers described in detail Kelly's childhood and her descent into a shady life. (Although reporters and authorities never treated it as a relevant detail, Kelly's ex-husband had been in Helena briefly during that autumn.) Kelly was buried in Helena's Forestvale Cemetery, and thereafter she was described or discussed infrequently in the unfolding investigation.

Through December, Montana newspapers regularly reported Jean Mills' fluctuating condition and prognoses. For a while Dr. Shearer expected infection from the bullet wounds to kill her—even when she appeared to be recovering. Although she was "delirious" by spells, Montana papers quoted Mills almost daily. Columnists applauded her deep interest in a son who lived in Denver with his grandmother, her $20,000 estate amassed for his care and education, and her fervent wish that he not be told how his mother earned her living.

On December 8, authorities arrested for Kelly's murder Nick Jancu—the "Nick" mentioned among Mills' early, confused explanations. Sheriff Burgess ordered the arrest after "tricking" Miss Mills into identifying Jancu as the murderer. In a move that no current court would sanction, Burgess arranged for Dr. Shearer to tell Jean that lawmen already "had the goods on" Jancu and had jailed him. Miss Mills—believing that her safety was secured—took the bait (*Helena Independent*, December 9, 1929): "Well, it was Nick who did it....He was all the time playing around with Bobby, and he said that he'd kill her sooner or later."

Newspapers identified Jancu as 34 years old, of Rumanian descent, and a World War I veteran who previously had been convicted of bootlegging. He had grown up on Nick Rorvig's sheep ranch in Broadwater County and currently owned a poolhall and a soft-drink parlor in Townsend. Police considered the handsome Jancu a "lady's man," and he attracted a courtroom of enamored young women during the trial. He was reported to have "financed" Bobby Kelly, visited her often, and frequently exhibited his violent temper and jealousy while in the Novelty Block.

Jancu stoutly denied any role in the murder. However, he did admit: to visiting Bobby on Sunday, December 1; to spending the evening drinking in Helena; to returning to Townsend so drunk on the morning of December 2 that he spent the day in bed. In an examination of Jancu, police could find no evidence of the bullet wounds that Mills thought she had inflicted seven days earlier. However, Mills reiterated her clear indictment of Jancu in a statement given to a court reporter on December 9.

Police also arrested George McDonald, Jancu's employee at the poolhall, who had spent the twenty-four hours preceding the crime with Jancu. Then, in one of the vignettes that makes this such a bizarre saga, Jean Mills announced that she would not testify against Jancu if he just would pay her doctor and hospital bills. Lawmen and the county attorney seemed to ignore this statement.

Nick Jancu's trial was postponed repeatedly while the prosecution waited for Jean Mills to recover. In early March, 1930, primary defense attorney Lester Loble finally insisted that District Judge W.H. Poorman proceed. The young Loble was assisted by Wilbur Eaton and Charles P. Cotter of Townsend. The prosecution's team consisted of County Attorney G.W. Padbury, Jr., and Deputy Attorneys A.P. Heywood and Sam D. Goza, Jr.

The jury selection took two days, as prosecutors weeded out candidates who opposed the death penalty or who proved staunchly critical of Kelly's lifestyle. The defense toiled to find people who knew none of the players and would not be swayed by Jean Mills' precarious health. The 12 jurors finally picked were—as in the summer gang trials—all men.

The trial's opening testimony involved few surprises and little drama. The state's witnesses outlined events in the same general pattern as the press had reported. Evidence involving bullets, bullet holes, angles of fire, bloody trails, and finger-prints remained as confusing and generally inconclusive as ever. Jurors were shown a diagram of the apartment and later taken there with Jancu in tow.

On March 7, the state produced Jean Mills, accompanied by two doctors and her nurse. The *Helena Independent* (March 8, 1930) reported that: "All the drama beneath the surface of the testimony, since the trial started, was released with the force of pent up waters upon a courtroom crowded to the limit of its capacity with spectators, most of whom were women." Jean offered roughly the same information that had been re-ported at the time of Jancu's arrest.

In his cross-examination, Defense Attorney Loble focused on her several earlier, contradictory statements. He painstak-ingly presented other men and incidents in Jean's life that might have triggered the crime. The prosecution wheeled Mills di-rectly in front of the jury, so they clearly could see her bullet wounds. Dr. Shearer then testified that her mental capacity and lucidity had not been reduced by the shooting. At the con-clusion of Miss Mills' testimony, the prosecution's case seemed viable, even strong.

Attorney Loble, however, changed the courtroom atmo-sphere with his opening defense statements and his initial call-ing of witnesses. Loble insisted that he could document Jan-cu's whereabouts on the evening of December 2 with phone records. Further, he could produce a veritable host of witness-es who would establish Jancu's presence in his poolhall when the murder occurred. He insisted that Jean Mills still suffered from mental defects that impaired her memory and judgment; he suggested that Jean likely was covering for someone else. He assured the jury that he could discredit any other evidence and witnesses brought by the prosecution.

Lester Loble's mannerisms alone implied drama, speed, and

intrigue. Then he accomplished much that he assured the jury he would. Judge Poorman sustained the prosecution's objection to introducing psychiatrists who would analyze Jean Mills' mental faculties. However, telephone-company employees documented a call that Jancu made from Townsend to Helena to his hunting partner Harry Lippert at 7:06 p.m. on Sunday, December 2.

Moreover, Loble paraded more than fifteen Townsend-area residents who insisted that they had seen Jancu at his poolhall/soft-drink parlor at various times between 5 P.M. and 8 P.M. on the evening of the murder. He also called a variety of character witnesses for Jancu, ranging from Helena and Townsend businessmen to county commissioners to county employees.

At this point, the trial became a veritable free-for-all. Colonel John J. McGuiness, court stenographer, was subpoenaed to present the notes that he had made in St. Peter's Hospital when Jean Mills first clearly identified Jancu as the murderer. McGuiness testified that those notes had been taken from his office and were nowhere to be found. County Attorney Padbury had no explanation for their disappearance.

As the prosecution quizzed Jancu's poolhall witnesses, it became obvious that few of them had frequented the poolhall before December 3—and some had never been there. The prosecution and the defense wrangled repeatedly about the time it might have taken Jancu to drive from Helena to Townsend on wintry, gravel roads.

The prosecution quizzed the character witnesses about Jancu's bootlegging conviction; the attorneys asked how that squared with Jancu's reputation for honesty and veracity. The witnesses responded (*Montana Record-Herald,* May 12, 1930) that they "didn't think that a conviction for bootlegging is considered a reflection on the reputation of a citizen of Broadwater County." George McDonald—Jancu's employee and companion on the December 1 night of revelry—had disappeared right after Jancu's arrest. He never was located or produced by either side.

In one compelling vignette, private investigator Henry Nelson told the jury that fingerprints he had found on a glass panel at the Novelty Block apartment were not Jancu's. But as examination and cross-examination continued, Nelson admitted that he had been paid for gathering evidence by both the state and the defense. And he revealed that he had not tried to match up the fingerprints with any of the several people who had been in the apartment during the investigation.

Further, two whiskey glasses seen by Police Sergeant Brown and the bottle of moonshine had disappeared from Kelly's apartment. Then a defense witness who admitted seeing Jancu's car close to the Townsend poolhall at the time of the murder admitted that he was color blind and could not really distinguish the Dodge Senior Six's blue body and red wheels.

Most confusing of all, Malcolm Grimes—one of several state witnesses produced to testify that he had seen Jancu in Helena at the time of the murder—contradicted the testimony he earlier had provided. The prosecution recalled Grimes from travels to Indiana for the trial. He began by asserting that he had seen Jancu on South Main Street during the late afternoon of Monday, December 2. Grimes testified that he had known Jancu and Kelly for some time. But subsequently Attorney Loble asked Grimes if he could recognize Jancu in the courtroom. Grimes leaned forward, looked directly at the defense table, and said, "No, I don't see him anywhere."

"The storm broke without warning. Women shouted and laughed and cheered with equal abandon. This was followed with a burst of handclapping. Men took part in the demonstration but their efforts were weak in comparison to the applause of the feminine delegation which made up nearly three-fourths of the audience" *(Helena Independent,* March 13, 1930).

Although Judge Poorman brought the courtroom back under control, the Grimes incident epitomized the community's mood and clearly foreshadowed the trial's outcome. While all of Montana watched, spectators crowded the galleries and brought lunches so they would not lose their seats. Women swooned over Jancu in his blue serge suit, green tie, and white shirt. Girls rushed him every day to shake his hand. A circus atmosphere pervaded the court proceedings because Jancu so obviously had become the scapegoat. Reality had taken flight; only the charade remained.

In its final statement, the prosecution warned the jury about an assortment of testimony based on possible perjury that the defense had offered. In so doing, the prosecution itself introduced "reasonable doubt." The jury retired to deliberate a 6 P.M. on March 14. It spent an hour eating dinner and was ready with its verdict by 7:30. Back in the courtroom at 8 P.M., the jury foreman announced a verdict of "not guilty." A group of Jancu's fans were present to celebrate; he gathered them up and went directly to a party.

On March 16, County Attorney Padbury informed the press that the Bobby Kelly murder likely would be listed as an "unsolved crime." On March 26, Jean Mills left for Denver with her nurse to see her son—the bullet fragments still in her skull.

So, did "the woman in white" know too much about the gang's summer crime spree and pay the ultimate price at the hands of a gang member? Or was Bobby Kelly's murder a tragic, but logical, conclusion to a life of alcohol and dissipation?

Given the sensationalism of the times and Bobby's occupation, did Montana enjoy this titillating drama more than it sought justice?

And finally, against America's background of 1920s and 1930s romanticized crime, what if reporter W.W. Casper's voice, proved the truest one? Remember Casper's words in the Helena *Montana Record-Herald* (March 12, 1930):

Behind the thin veil that separates the known from the unknown in the Margaret (Bobby) Kelly murder case, there surges a score of shadowy figures, barely discernible,…

These figures are silent as the tomb. They flit swiftly to and fro, and from their passings emanates a cold, menacing breath like that from some dismal morass. They are on the "inside" and… learn in advance what the next move will be. They have influences in high places; they pull strings and puppets move to do their bidding. Their shadows fall like the chill of cold steel, and warm flesh trembles. But their identities are never revealed.

Should Casper's "thin veil" continued to shield the silent, shadowy, malevolent figures behind the Bobby Kelly murder?

Will their identities never be revealed?

MOUNT ST. CHARLES FOOTBALL 1931

BY DAVE WALTER

A portion of Helena's unique "character" depends on its outstanding sports teams. For example, the Helena High girls' basketball team that won the 1991 state tournament, the Capital High squad that took the state AA football crown in 1993, and the 1995 Helena Brewers team that captured the Pioneer League championship all recently have contributed to the community's special "character."

Yet one Helena sports team stands head-and-shoulders above the rest: the 1931 Mount Saint Charles football eleven. In a era of thin padding, no face masks, infrequent forward passes, and men who played *both offense and defense,* the unpretentious team from Helena's Catholic college proved supreme. The "Hilltoppers" (at that time only occasionally called the "Saints") crafted a season from which they emerged *undefeated, untied, and unscored upon!*

They took on all comers from Montana's collegiate ranks— including Montana State College in Bozeman and Montana State University in Missoula—and gained the title of "Montana State Collegiate Football Champs." In a season of astounding accomplishment, the Mount Saint Charles team flirted with immortality—and with magic.

Certainly in September of 1931 (smack in the middle of a deepening national Depression), nothing indicated that the Mount Saint Charles football program held the slightest promise. Wilbur Eaton, coach of the team since 1926, had left the team. School officials scrambled to hire Bill Jones at the last minute. Jones had coached the Notre Dame University freshman team in 1930 and arrived in Helena highly recommended.

Jones, however, counted just six returning lettermen from a 1930 team that had won only a single game, lost four, and tied one. In addition, the school had signed an intercollegiate cost-cutting agreement that permitted it to practice only *five days* prior to its first game. Although about forty students from the all-male school turned out for the first practice on September 15, Coach Jones realized that he faced formidable odds to improve the team's 1930 record.

The inexperienced purple-and-gold's first test came on September 20, when it faced the Centerville Independents, a club team from Butte that mixed hardrock miners and professional players. Under coach Vivian Burr, a former Hilltopper, this squad of huge linemen and swift backs had been practicing for three full weeks. Nevertheless the Mount Saint Charles team that took rain-soaked Scullon Field more than countered that experience with enthusiasm. (Scullon Field—sporting wooden bleachers and surrounded by an eight-foot board fence—sat on the north end of the college campus, approximately on the current site of the Carroll College Physical Education Center.)

Despite an inexperienced line and the inability to kick an extra point, the Hilltoppers emerged with a 20-0 victory. Charles "Chick" Garner carried the offense *(Helena Daily Independent,* September 21, 1931): "The shifty Garner gave some excellent exhibitions of broken-field running. Three of his brilliant dashes won a hearty roar from the shivering spectators as he stepped, dodged, and twisted his way for long gains, scoring all three of the team's touchdowns."

Yet Coach Jones had little time to celebrate, as the next weekend he led the Mount Saint Charles eleven into Missoula to face an accomplished Montana State University team. The Hilltoppers had never defeated the powerful University. The Grizzlies had won the 1930 game 52-0 and had embarrassed Mount Saint Charles 133-0 in 1920. But the University also suffered from the five-practice agreement, and Coach Bernie Oakes feared meeting the Hilltoppers in his first game.

He should have worried! In a stunning upset, David stoned

Goliath 2-0! *(Montana Record-Herald,* September 28, 1931):

For the first time in history, a Montana Grizzly hide is hanging in the trophy room of a small school that stands on a hilltop here. The upset left Grizzly supporters blinking and Hilltopper backers asking for confirmation of the score.

A safety, scored on a bad pass from center in the first quarter, provided Saint Charles with the margin they grimly defended. A plodding Montana team threatened several times, losing the ball on downs at the Hilltoppers' 3-yard line in the fourth quarter, muffing forward passes three times on the Saint Charles' 10-yard line, and fumbling in the final minutes on the Helena 20-yard line.

The University outplayed their opponent, making 16 first downs to the Hilltoppers' 3, but Saint Charles showed a superior fighting spirit, determination, and dash, and fought in spectacular fashion to maintain its lead.

Coach Jones brought his players back to earth with exhausting practices during the next two weeks. On October 10 the Hilltoppers faced crosstown rival Intermountain Union in the Panthers' first game of the season. (The Intermountain Union campus sat approximately on the current site of the Capital Hill Mall. After the 1935 earthquakes, the college affiliated with Billings Polytechnic Institute and moved to Billings. In 1947 the two schools merged to form Rocky Mountain College.)

Officials postponed kickoff time until 3:00, so fans could listen to the final game of the World Series between the St. Louis Cardinals and the Philadelphia Athletics on the radio. Once the game began before a crowd of several thousand, however, Saint Charles thrashed the Panthers 62-0. An injury in practice to "Chick" Garner kept him out of the game and mercifully benefitted the Intermountaineers.

The Montana Normal School in Dillon represented the next hurdle in Mount Saint Charles' quest for the "Montana Collegiate Championship." Despite Garner's continued absence, the Hilltoppers trounced the future teachers 83-0. The victors re-

The 1931 Mount Saint Charles team. Top row: End coach Sid Smith, James Cronin, Ben Evans, Tony Niklas, Eugene Dunnigan, Thomas O'Connor, Frank Harrington, Coleman Mulligan, Adolph Zuelke. Center: Coach Bill Jones, George Doyle, Albert Donich, Louis Dvorsky, Fred Fox, Frank May, James Conway, Bradley Seeley, trainer George Moses, assistant coach John Good. Front: Philip Davidson, William Nugent, Raymond Botch, Walter Mack, co-captain Larry Scheewe, co-captain Chick Garner, Clarence Mayer, Donald Snyder, John McGillis, James Freebourn.

lied on long end runs and bewildering reverses for several of their scores. Four games into their season, Saint Charles remained undefeated, had scored 167 points, and had allowed no opponent to cross its goal line!

Coach Jones next anticipated a stern test when the team faced the Montana School of Mines Orediggers at Clark Park in Butte. He commented, "The boys and I hold no foolish ideas about the strength of the Orediggers, and we will go into Butte prepared to shoot the works at them!"

Led by a healthy "Chick" Garner, the Hilltoppers capitalized on two Oredigger fumbles and scored three times to defeat the School of Mines 19-0. Immediately following the shutout, Coach Jones focused the team's attention on its final game against the Montana State College Bobcats in Helena on Armistice (Veterans) Day.

With the "Montana Collegiate Championship" hanging in the balance, the Hilltoppers held two-and-one-half weeks of grueling practices prior to this homecoming game. The Montana American Legion planned to sponsor the game as the key event in its statewide veterans' celebration. At Scullon Field, college crews erected 1,000 additional bleacher seats hauled in from Butte. Helena merchants agreed to close for the afternoon of the holiday game; Helena public schools also would dismiss early. Requests for tickets poured into the college from all across the state, and "special" trains prepared to run from Great Falls, Butte, and Bozeman for the game.

In key psychological moves, Coach Jones appointed "Chick" Garner captain for the team's last game and then closed his practices to the press. Montana State officials countered by sending a carload of their most ostentatious football trophies to be displayed in the window of the A.M. Holter Hardware Store. Mount Saint Charles authorities then announced that all children in the state's several orphanages would be admitted to the game free—and the offer gained statewide public support for the college.

On Tuesday evening, the all-male student body of Mount Saint Charles (many clad in colorful pajamas) snake-danced through downtown Helena to the campus. The frenzied homecoming marchers were led by the Helena High band and joined

MOUNT SAINT CHARLES HILLTOPPERS: 1931

NUMBER	NAME	POSITION	HOME TOWN
1	Leary Mills	halfback	Garden Valley
2*	James Freebourn	quarterback	Butte
3*	Raymond Botch	end	Wibaux
4	Jack McDonald	tackle	Helena
5	Philip Botch	guard	Wibaux
6*	Frank May	center	Havre
7	George Doyle	guard	Miles City
8*	Philip Davidson	halfback	Anaconda
9*	Donald Snyder	quarterback	North Platte
10*	Ben Evans	end	Helena
11*	Anthony Nicklas	halfback	Helena
12*	Thomas O'Connor	halfback	Miles City
13*	William Nugent	quarterback	Miles City
14*	Frank Harrington	end	Butte
15*	James Cronin	guard	Sioux City
16*	Walter Mack	halfback	Havre
17*	Eugene Dunnigan	center	Miles City
18*	Matt MacMahon	fullback	Havre
19*	John McGillis	halfback	Deer Lodge
20	Adolph Zuelkhe	guard	Helena
21*	Coleman Mulligan	end	Anaconda
22	William Sullivan	guard	Butte
23*	Bradley Seeley	end	Helena
4*	Louis Dvorsky	tackle	Iowa City
25*	James Conway	end	Livingston
26*	Larry Scheewe	halfback	Helena
27*	Arthur Doyle	guard	Miles City
28	Gene Connors	center	Townsend
29*	Fred Fox	tackle	Hollywood
30	John O'Neil	guard	Butte
31	Joseph Laux	tackle	Lewistown
32*	Clarence Mayer	guard	Havre
33*	Charles Garner	halfback	Pocatello
34	Floyd Mayer	tackle	Polson
35*	Albert Donich	tackle	Deer Lodge
36	Warren Nelson	end	Great Falls
37	Edward Foley	halfback	Butte
38	Rector Budell	guard	Philipsburg
39	John Johnston	tackle	Idaho Falls
40	Donald Nash	halfback	Bozeman

1931 letter winners

by hundreds of townspeople. Near Scullon Field the crowd of more than 1,000 assembled around a monstrous pyre *(The Prospector*, December 17, 1931):

> *For weeks previous the freshmen class had been collecting all the available material that could be found in Helena, from old packing boxes to choice railroad ties. A large base of railroad ties was built and into this enclosure truck after truck discharged its load of paper and boxes, and the pile rose higher and higher. Guards were placed the previous night to insure safety.*
>
> *But as the morning of November tenth dawned, things looked very black, for the Northern Pacific Railroad demanded the return of their ties. Woe the poor freshmen! To remove the ties from the base meant the ruination of their fire. Diplomats were sent to the railroad officials, and they succeeded in persuading the railroad company that they should give their ties to a noble cause. The pile was soaked with oil. All was now in readiness—even to the outhouse containing the "Bobcat," which perched atop the pile.*
>
> A rousing cheer. The freshmen lit the pyre. As the flames reached their zenith, Coach Jones delivered a short speech to the pep-rally crowd. "Revelers who turned their eyes toward Mount Helena saw the college's 'C' beautifully illuminated with red flames." *(The Prospector*, December 17, 1931)

CARROLL COLLEGE

Quarterback Don Snyder.

On the morning of November 11, a few last tickets went on sale at the Higgins Cigar Store and at the Rialto downtown. The crisp, windy November weather cooperated, and the game was an absolute sellout, with the crowd estimated at more than 2,500 fans.

In keeping with all of the excitement and publicity, the Hilltopper-Bobcat contest developed into a nail-biter. At its conclusion, Mount Saint Charles emerged a 6-0 victor, on the strength of "Chick" Garner's consecutive, second-quarter runs of 32, 15, and 2 yards into the end zone. Thereafter a defensive, field-position battle ensued: Garner punted eighteen times for the Hilltoppers; Bobcat George Parke punted thirteen times. The gusty wind caused the Bobcats to complete only four of sixteen passes. In the end, the Saint Charles goal line remained inviolate.

Against all logic and odds, the 1931 football team from tiny Mount Saint Charles captured the title of "Montana State Collegiate Football Champions." The purple-and-gold shut out all of its opponents, while scoring 192 points themselves. The *Montana Record-Herald* concluded (November 12, 1931):

> *It has been quite a season for the Hilltop college and one of which the school as well as the people of Helena can be proud. The men comprising the team were not all experienced at the opening of the season, and Coach Bill Jones had to do a lot of work to whip his material into the smooth-running machine he led at the end of play. He had an enthusiastic lot, and this coupled with his skill in developing players brought glory to the college and pride to the townspeople. We have, simply, the best football team in the state right here in Helena!*

Still smarting from its 2-0 defeat at the hands of the Hilltoppers, Montana State University officials tried to entice Mount Saint Charles into a rematch in Missoula "with the proceeds of the game to be donated to charities that benefit the unemployed." The champions respectfully declined and preserved their crown. They deserved to bask in the glory that a David-and-Goliath victor receives—for they constituted Helena's greatest athletic team.

THOMAS WALSH, HELENA LAWYER

BY RICHARD B. ROEDER

In 1890 there arrived in Helena an ambitious small town lawyer from Redfield, South Dakota. His name was Thomas J. Walsh. Walsh was born June 12, 1859 in Two Rivers, Wisconsin of Irish immigrant parents. A public school education followed by teaching and much reading on his own enabled him to attend the University of Wisconsin Law School from which he received an LLB in 1884. After establishing a moderately adequate practice, he married Elinor McClements in 1889.

Walsh and Elinor discussed the fees lawyers commanded in Montana compared to his country practice. They decided that he should try to cut into the market and chose to start in Helena which would be his home

Thomas Walsh, ca. 1925.

for the rest of his life. The move proved to be a smart one. With Elinor, who soon established her own reputation as a woman's rights advocate, working with her husband in the law office, their practice grew steadily. Although he never accumulated great wealth, Walsh typically broadened his interests to include mining, ranching, and part ownership of the *Helena Independent*. Within a few years he was able to move his family form a modest home on Lawrence Street to a mansion he had built at 343 Clarke Street, currently owned and occupied by Steve and Judy Browning.

Walsh prepared cases with meticulous care. He soon acquired a reputation as an outstanding lawyer, especially in mining and constitutional law. He also became known as a defender of workers in industrial accident cases at a time when the common law stacked the deck against the working man. At mid-career, he turned down an offer to be general counsel for the Anaconda Company.

Walsh was a staunch Democrat, and his standing within the party rose steadily as he worked on behalf of the party from precinct to county levels. His first attempt at public office came in 1906 when he ran unsuccessfully for the state's lone seat in the U.S. House of Representatives. He also lost a bid for a Senate seat in 1910, but in 1912, he defeated Joseph Dixon under Montana's Senate preference law. He remained in the Senate until 1933.

At first blush it seems unlikely that he should be a successful politician since he was nothing like the outgoing, glad-handing office seeker. Publicly he appeared austere and humorless. His photographs, even those used for campaign purposes, reveal a man with a heavy moustache glowering into the camera with piercing eyes. His political speeches were not designed to be crowd pleasers. They were carefully researched, full of facts, and presented without flair. Of his 1906 house race, a Missoula reporter noted that a speech in that city was "strong, ponderous somewhat, and in its airiest flights it was rather the gambol of a pachyderm than the soaring of an eagle." Newspapers generally referred to his aloofness and lack of popular appeal.

What, then, were the sources of strength of this uncommon politician? Largely they were party loyalty, his prowess as a lawyer and his unshakable personal integrity. He was a constant worker for the Democratic Party. He attended every national convention from 1904 to 1932 and was chairman of both the 1928 and 1932 conventions. His reputation as a lawyer secured him great respect. The sense of order with which he prepared his cases was a salient feature of his character revealed by his dress and speech. One reporter noted that "It would be equal relief to hear him split an infinitive as see him with his neckties awry." This same imperturbable sense of rightness also set Walsh apart from the political crowd. A reporter commented that to ask Walsh for a political favor "would be like asking the statue of Civic Virtue for a chew of tobacco."

In Washington, Walsh's reputation grew in a Senate that included such luminaries as Robert M. La Follette, George Norris, Hiram Johnson, and William E. Borah. His rise was delayed following his wife Elinor's death in 1917. After her funeral on September 4, Walsh went into a deep depression and family and friends kept him incommunicado for about a year. He was catapulted into national fame by his role in uncovering the scandals of the Harding administration. Walsh headed the Senate committee that revealed oil lease frauds at Tea Pot Dome, Wyoming, and elsewhere. The upshot of Walsh's work was that Secretary of Interior Albert B. Fall was convicted of fraud, subjected to a heavy fine, and imprisoned for a year. From this point on Walsh received national recognition. On several occasions the press speculated about a Supreme Court appointment and on May 4, 1925 his photo appeared on the cover of *Time* magazine. In 1928, he announced his candidacy for president as a dry, but after the California primaries he withdrew in favor of Al Smith, a wet on prohibition.

Walsh's reputation was as a strong liberal. By today's standards this label does not seem warranted. He opposed early conservation policies and regarded Theodore Roosevelt and Gifford Pinchot, first director of the Forest Service, as eastern busybodies who did not understand western problems and interfered with property rights. His enthusiasm for irrigation and development generally included his hearty support of dam construction, including one well within the boundaries of Yellowstone National Park. He was an Indian assimilationist who worked to open reservations to white settlement. His fear of the Industrial Workers of the World during World War I gained his support for a national sedition law and the raids of attorney Mitchell Palmer. He refused to support reappointment of his friend Burton K. Wheeler as federal district attorney because of Wheeler's support by radical groups in Montana.

The Walsh home at 343 Clarke Street in Helena.

On the other hand, Walsh was a consistent supporter of the causes of the working man, a support that went back to the beginning of his career. He believed that unemployment was a problem to be dealt with by Congress, which ought to accept responsibility for full employment. He believed that all Americans were entitled to a decent standard of living. He was an avid supporter of President Wilson's national reforms. He changed his mind on civil liberty issues and became a critic of the Supreme Court and defender of individual liberties. He was a leading advocate of confirmation of Louis Brandeis for the Supreme Court against an opposition based on veiled anti-semitism. He supported constitutional amendments for women's suffrage and outlawing child labor, and he backed voting rights for blacks. A constant in his life was his fear of the growing power of private corporations in public affairs.

Public approval of Walsh is clearly revealed by the fact that in 1930 appreciative Montanans placed a marble bust of him in one of the niches in the state capitol rotunda where it remained until rashly moved to make way for a trashy plaque commemorating the 1989 Centennial Commission. The climax of Walsh's career came in 1933.

His reputation as a lawyer and man of integrity justified President Roosevelt's appointment of him as attorney general, the only Montanan ever to be appointed to a full cabinet post. Unfortunately, he did not live to assume office. On February 25, 1933, Walsh married an attractive Cuban widow considerably younger than he. Walsh died with his bride at his side March 2, on a train to Washington to be sworn in. One would like to believe that the ever austere cabinet appointee died with a smile on his face.

Walsh's body lay in the Senate for a memorial service attended by President Roosevelt, the cabinet, and diplomatic corps. In his eulogy of his colleague and friend, Senator Wheeler said Walsh was the "most distinguished citizen Montana has developed." Walsh's body then lay in the state capitol rotunda while approximately 10,000 passed in view. Walsh had been a very active Catholic layman who supported Carroll College and Helena's parochial schools. It is hardly surprising that some 2,000 packed St. Helena Cathedral for the funeral mass. He is buried in Resurrection Cemetery.

PLACES

RODNEY STREET

BY HARRIETT C. MELOY

Today, Rodney Street measures one and three-quarters miles from Acropolis to Lyndale. The street was named in 1868 for Dr. Rodney Pococke, who died in 1865, the first person to draw his last breath in the mining camp.

In the early 1870s, miners and business people perceived Rodney Street as an obvious choice for a new center of business and residential activity in Helena because Main and Jackson streets, developed from the camp's first days, had grown drastically crowded. Businesses from banks to laundries were springing up overnight, and no space remained in the narrow gulch.

To add to the Gulch's growth problems, log cabins were

The H.M. Parchen home at 207 South Rodney burned down in the early 1930s.

interspersed with businesses, because miners often built dwellings close to their work, even though that practice created certain risks. Lizzie Fisk, wife of the *Helena Herald* editor, described one such hazard in a letter to her mother in Connecticut. She told how one miner's lady stepped out her back door and fell down a five foot shaft that had been dug in the early morning hours of that same day.

The young mining camp's physical growth was wholly dependent on its topographical features. To the west, Mount Helena's steep slope forbade developing in that direction. To the east, beyond Rodney Street, was deep Dry Gulch, which discouraged the laying out of new streets and homes. It's no wonder that Rodney Street's wide flat area—"the center of a ridge that separates Last Chance Gulch from Davis"—was viewed as ideal for the mining community's development.

Directly west of Rodney, also on the ridge, sat the new Court House where all official business was conducted. Many employees lived in apartments and rooming houses in the area. Grocery stores and livery stables sprang up nearby to serve the burgeoning population. A holding stable for parade horses used for special government celebrations was built at 200 North Rodney. It can still be recognized today by the decorative 19th century cornice above the stucco facade. Next door, at 211, is a small rooming house that was maintained by the Catholic church for visiting friends. One of these friends was said to be Louis Riel, the charismatic leader of the Métis people, who lived in Montana between 1883 and 1885, just before he returned to Canada and was hanged for treason.

In spite of intense activity surrounding the Court House and new jail, the residential potential of Rodney Street was attractive to prominent Helena citizens. A list of these Helenans may well begin with China Clarke, partner of Clarke, Conrad and Curtin, who established one of the earliest important wholesale houses. Clarke erected his palatial Italianate style home at 207 South Rodney Street in the 1870s. One of the first and finest examples of striking Victorian architecture in the city, the building burned in the early 1930s while it was home to the H.M. Parchen family. A modern bungalow sits on the corner lot today, bordered by the original stone wall.

Further down the street, Martin Holter's Second Empire style home, built in 1879 at 15 North Rodney Street, appears much as it did over a century ago. Martin was the brother of the better known entrepreneur, Anton M. Holter.

At 28 North Rodney, across the street from Holter's residence, Michael Reinig built a handsome home. Its architecture with mansard roof was similar to Holter's. Reinig arrived in Helena in 1866 and became a successful grocer and wine merchant. In 1992, his home was razed to make room for car parking.

Joseph K. Toole, one of the territory's most brilliant lawyers, built at 74 South Rodney in 1870. He later moved across State Street to 102 South Rodney. After he became Montana's first state governor in 1889, he and his family occupied the handsome Ewing Street mansion opposite the Chessman apartments.

A couple of blocks away, also in 1870, Robert E. Fisk, the well-known and at times controversial editor of the *Helena Herald,* built his residence at 319 North Rodney. Frame rather than brick or stone, the home still stands today. The Fisks' neighbor was territorial governor James Ashley, who held office only a few months. Another territorial governor, Preston H. Leslie, lived in

A Fourth of July parade passes a rooming house on the corner of Breckenridge and Rodney.

the same immediate neighborhood. He resided on the southeast corner of Sixth and Rodney for a short while before he moved to his more permanent address on Ewing.

In the next block the Queen Anne style Silverman home was built at 412 North Rodney in 1880. The residence was and is one of the most imposing dwellings on the street. Morris Silverman came to Helena in 1867 and began a prosperous mercantile business. Later the uncle of Moz J. Silverman (see page 31), he was a member of the city council for years, belonged to several Masonic lodges and served as president of the Jewish lodge for three terms.

The highly successful wholesale and retail druggist, Francis Pope, built his handsome dwelling at 327 North Rodney in 1889. Today the well-preserved building is an antique shop.

August Fack was owner of Main Street's most popular gathering place in the 19th century, the California Wine House. He built his home in 1890 at 556 South Rodney, high up on the hill. Though Fack's name is not mentioned in any of the state histories, he was recognized as one of the few Helena art aficionados of the day. Several original Robert Swaim paintings decorated the walls of his home, and for his wine house he purchased a white marble statue from Italy. The figure, "a danc-

The Michael Reinig home at 28 South Rodney.

ing girl wearing thin drapery," was bought for $7,200 in 1900, and stunningly arranged in Fack's bar with maroon velvet drapes and "veiled lighting."

Although other worthy and engaging homes deserve notice, it seems appropriate, while describing the history of Rodney Street, to at least mention the several "first" schools scattered along the distinguished route. Which school actually was "the first" was debatable over the years.

To begin, the first "first" school was opened by Professor A.B. Patch in 1865 in his own home, but no record exists as to the exact location, except that it was on Rodney. Twelve to twenty students attended.

Professor T.F. Campbell started the second "first" school in 1866 on the corner of Rodney and State, where China Clarke built his mansion a few years later. The third "first" school was constructed in 1868 on the site that Michael Reinig's home eventually occupied. Presumably a good-sized frame structure, the school accommodated fifty pupils.

All of these schools charged tuition. But in 1890 the first public school, Emerson, was built at 519 South Rodney. Made of brick, the three-story edifice came down after the 1935 earthquakes; a new one-story school arose in 1942, and was named for well-loved educator Mae Butler.

Many of the original residences and the school remain today, undaunted by more than a century's wear and tear. After the beginning of the 20th century, no palatial mansions were built along Rodney. For one reason, desirable residential land was not available. Yet another reason was that banks ceased loaning money to home builders who hoped to locate above State Street on Rodney; the proximity of the infamous Wood Street had made the area seem an unlikely investment. Perhaps the greatest reason was the exodus to the West Side, which began in 1885, after Samuel T. Hauser built his twenty-nine–room mansion on Madison Avenue. People with prestige and bankrolls followed.

Rodney Street has always maintained a character that sets it off from other Helena thoroughfares. Even today, current and past residents alike speak fondly of Rodney Street as their favorite neighborhood.

Central Park on Ten Mile Creek

By Vivian A. Paladin

The name Central Park conjures up memories for many people still living as an almost magical place for having fun. Situated on Ten Mile Creek on the western outskirts of Helena, the spacious grounds contained such things as a merry-go-round, a large outdoor dance pavilion, two restaurants, two saloons, a lake used for boating in the summer and for ice harvesting in the winter, bowling alleys, a league-size baseball field with grandstand, picnic areas, a zoo with all kinds of animals and birds, including peacocks and white swans that were allowed to roam the grounds at will.

MONTANA HISTORICAL SOCIETY

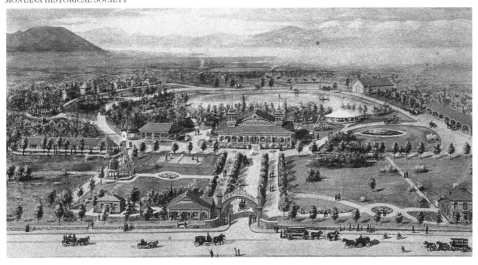

Central Park's dance pavilion.

When Central Park was opened to the public in 1895, it became an important part of a legendary complex on Helena's western edge, all served by an electric trolley system. There was C. A. Broadwater's Hotel and Natatorium, opened in 1889, Nick Kessler's Brewery and brickyard that had been serving the growing city's needs for refreshment and building materials since the mid-1880s, and Tom Mills' State Nursery, still in operation today but in its infant years when it took on the awesome task of landscaping the grounds of both the Broadwater and Central Park.

Barely discernible remains of the splendid Broadwater and Natatorium molder on the grounds that Mills lavishly planted and maintained, and drastic changes have taken place at Kessler's brewery and brickyard, the latter now serving as site of the nationally known Archie Bray Foundation, center for ceramic arts.

Central Park, built by two visionary brothers, Joseph and Frank Mares, lives on as well but in a different guise. Since 1943, it has been the site of the Green Meadow Country Club. Many of the trees Tom Mills planted still line the fairways and shade the grounds of the clubhouse. Dedicated groundskeepers watch over the trees, prune and nurture them and promptly replace them when they finally die.

A stone fence, fashioned of bluestone rock, still partially surrounds the front of the property. It was the work of Ernest Mares, son of one of the founders of Central Park, who recalled not long ago that he was an eighteen-year-old when he hand-picked the rock and hauled it to the site with a wagon and a team of horses.

Information about this extraordinary place and its founders has been provided in large measure, in fact, by Ernest Mares, who has lived for many years in Webster Groves, Missouri. He has returned for several nostalgic visits and has been a generous correspondent with those who have sought information about the place where he grew up.

The story, as it turns out, encompasses much more than an amusement park, for the Mares brothers, both born in what was once part of the Austro-Hungarian Empire, were innovative and enterprising businessmen. As will be seen, they developed a major retail meat market business in Helena and a complex for meat storage and processing as well as the Central Park facilities for recreation suitable for people of all ages.

Ernest's father, Joseph, was born in 1856 and came to this country in 1876. Settling first in Cedar Rapids, Iowa, he came to Montana in 1878 and was soon engaged in harnessmaking and open range horse-raising near Fort Benton. In 1880, he bought part interest in a ranch that extended from Square Butte near Cascade to the Sun River, and in the meantime, worked at his craft of making harnesses, saddles, and articles of clothing from leather and fur, selling them throughout the territory. By the 1880s, he had established a retail business in Marysville.

Frank Mares, born in Bohemia in 1862, joined his brother in Montana in about 1882, working at his butcher trade in Helena. In about 1890, using profits made from some investments in mining, Joseph moved to Helena, where he and Frank bought out, in partnership with Henry Fisher, the Scheewe and Parker Meat Market on Warren Street, renaming it the Mares and Fisher Meat Market. In 1892, this flourishing business moved to larger quarters on Broadway, and changed its name to the Central Meat Market. Finally, its long-time name, the Helena Meat Company, was adopted. Its final location was on the east side of Main Street, just north of the intersection of Sixth and Main.

It was their growing meat business that led the Mares brothers to seek out some acreage out of town on which to build a place for handling cattle and processing meat. In 1892, when they heard that some acreage known as Kranick's Grove was up for sheriff's sale, they acted promptly to buy it, for although it was much larger than they needed for the meat business, it was ideal. The tracks of the Northern Pacific cut right through the property, and on the north side of the tracks there was plenty of room for a slaughter house, ice-cooled and insulated meat storage, a stable and pasturage for horses, a feedlot for cattle, housing for employees, and even a cookhouse.

On the south side of the tracks, the brothers decided to build an amusement park, a facility much needed in a city growing in sophistication and population. They first called the place Mares Park but soon renamed it Central Park. Construction began almost immediately and major facilities, including the dance pavilion, were ready for the grand opening in 1895.

"Shortly after Central Park opened," Ernest Mares wrote in 1986, "the Northern Pacific was interested in showing railroad passengers big game: buffalo, elk, deer, etc. A high-wire fence was built along the railroad right-of-way for this purpose. The passenger trains would slow down—sometimes stop—to give passengers a close-up look..."

In describing more fully the zoo at Central Park, Mares wrote that in addition to the native wild animals along the railroad, his father had built on the grounds of the amusement park a domed aviary to house birds of many kinds, with cages for monkeys, bears, and coyotes, and open pens for rabbits.

Central Park had been open to the public less than three years when Governor Robert B. Smith issued a call early in May 1898 for a regiment of Montana volunteers for service in the Spanish-American War. In a flurry of patriotism, hundreds volunteered and were ordered to rendezvous in Helena between May 6 and 8 and set up camp at Central Park, to be renamed

Camp Smith in honor of the governor. The recruits were housed in hundreds of rented tents and improvised quarters in the dance pavilion.

Things got really hectic at Camp Smith on Sunday, May 15, when five special trains came to Helena from all over Montana carrying some 3,000 visitors, most of them relatives of the volunteers. The *Helena Herald* said restaurants ran out of food, while trolleys and hacks failed to accommodate all those who wanted to visit loved ones at the camp. Many people walked. To add to the confusion, it began raining in the afternoon and continued to rain for days. Drills continued, however, with surgeons busily vaccinating for smallpox, immunizing some 500 men a day. It was not long before Central Park and its military occupants were so bogged down in mud that Camp Smith had to be moved to higher ground just west of the Broadwater School, south of the Great Northern tracks.

Under the command of Colonel Harry Kessler, the regiment completed its training late in May. As they lined up to be shipped out for duty in the Philippines, the Mares brothers presented the men with an American eagle from the Central Park menagerie to serve as a mascot. The bird was named Dewey.

After the troops left, activities at Central Park and the meat processing facilities across the tracks returned to normal. The brothers went on with their lives, and indeed married sisters. In September 1899, Joseph married Antoinette Yama in Omaha, and they returned immediately to Helena. They became the parents of three children, Lillian, Joseph and Ernest, all of whom were born at the family's red brick home on the grounds of Central Park. Frank married Antoinette's younger sister, Emma, in April 1901, the wedding taking place in the parlor of the Mares home at Central Park. They became the parents of a daughter, Blanche, who lived out her life in Helena.

During a mid-1990s visit to Helena, Ernest Mares said it was hard to realize that the house where he lived as a boy has been replaced by a parking lot. "But I was happy to see," he said, "that the bluestone fence I put up in 1925 is still intact and in reasonably good shape. Overall, I am gratified that the Green Meadow Country Club has maintained and improved these grounds where so many wonderful things have happened."

The Little Prickly Pear Valley

By Jon Axline

Historically, Helena has been the center of an extensive transportation, mining and agricultural network. Some of the communities surrounding the Capital City, however, were important in their own right and significant to Helena's survival. The Little Prickly Pear Valley is a vital, and often overlooked, component of Helena's history and development.

The valley was first visited by Euro-Americans in the 1830s. Working for either the American Fur Company or the Hudson's Bay Company, a small group of French-Canadian trappers had settled in the Little Prickly Pear Valley by 1845. The location of the settlement is not known.

In 1858, John Mullan's military road crossed the valley near Montana Al's Silver City Bar. It was not until gold was discovered at Silver Creek five years later that the valley was permanently settled.

William Mayger discovered gold on Silver Creek in 1862. There are two accounts of how the creek was named. The first states that it was named for the high silver content of the placer gold in the stream. The second claims the creek was named for a nearby homesteader named "Silver." Regardless of how it was named, the richest gold-bearing gravel was located in the terraces above the creek. The miners had to haul the gravel nearly a mile before it could be washed through the sluice boxes.

Within a few weeks of the discovery, Silver City had a population of fifty people and included "the usual wagon store, shanty saloon and [brush] wakiups...." When gold was discovered on Grasshopper Creek later that year, most of the miners working along Silver Creek abandoned their claims and Silver City became one of Montana's earliest ghost towns.

Mayger and his partner George Detweiler reopened the Silver Creek mines in 1864. Like a phoenix, Silver City rose from the ashes and once again served as an important mining camp. Although later eclipsed by the gold strike on Last Chance Gulch, Silver City had a population of 108 men and was, for a few months, the first county seat of Lewis and Clark County (then called Edgerton County).

By September of 1864, however, the discovery of gold on Last Chance Gulch drew many of the Silver Creek miners away to the more easily worked and higher grade placers. By 1870, only sixty-four men were still working what had become marginal placer and quartz mines. In a last-ditch attempt to extract as much as they could from the glacial till bordering the creek, the miners began the dangerous process of drift mining the gravel. Because of frequent and potentially deadly cave-ins and the low returns, the mines were eventually abandoned in favor of the new strikes in the hills surrounding Marysville. Remnants of the gold placers can be seen adjacent to Birdseye Road near the junction with Secondary Highway 279.

Silver "City" had twenty-five inhabitants, of which only five were miners, in 1880. By this time, Silver City had ceased being an important mining center and, instead, became a hub for the transportation system that connected the valley to Fort Benton, Helena and Lincoln. When the Montana Central Railroad arrived in 1886, the community relocated to take advantage of the opportunities afforded by the railroad. Old Silver City was located just southeast of Montana Al's Silver City Bar.

Information about the Trinity Creek mines is vague at best. Gold was discovered on the creek in 1865 or 1866. In 1870, Trinity City boasted a population of 116 people, including twelve women. Before the boom ended in 1872, the little gold camp contained thirty-nine buildings with a total assessed value of $6,200.

An 1871 map of the area shows a small community located just southwest of the Trinity Creek bridge on Secondary Highway 279, about 2½ miles southeast of the Canyon Creek Store. By 1880, however, the camp could claim only forty-nine occu-

William Mayger.

pants, most of whom were farming and ranching the area around the old placer mines.

The county apportioned $416.22 to the settlement for the education of Trinity City's children. A school was built for that purpose and eventually moved to Canyon Creek. Today, Trinity City itself has long since disappeared and all that remains are the scarred stream bed and the placer tailings adjacent to the highway.

The true value of the Little Prickly Pear Valley was in the fertile soil and its location on an important transportation route. Marysville and the Stemple Pass mines provided a lucrative market for the farmers and ranchers living in the valley.

In 1870, thirty-nine people lived in the valley near Canyon Creek. Most of them were placer miners and only one individ-

The Silver City stage station in 1918.

ual worked as a rancher. Within a decade, however, eighty-one people (including fifteen families) lived near Canyon Creek; half of them were European immigrants employed in the agricultural industry.

The 160-acre homesteads provided wheat and potatoes to the residents of the mining camps and to consumers in Helena. Many Helena businessmen, such as Herman Ganz and Joseph Klein, also established small ranches in the valley in the late 1860s. Ganz's 200-acre sheep and cattle ranch was among the largest in the valley.

During the 1890s and early 1900s, local farmers and ranchers supplemented their incomes by building primitive cyanide mills to recover gold from the tailings that drifted down Silver, Trinity and Little Prickly Pear creeks from the mines in the mountains. It is not known how much gold was recovered from the tailings using this process or where exactly the cyanide mills were located.

Although production from the hard rock mines waned after 1900, agricultural production in the valley continued to expand until 1923, partly because of the presence of a good road system to facilitate the movement of goods to local markets.

In 1870, William Negus established a toll road from Silver City to the new gold camp of Lincoln (Secondary 279 roughly parallels the old toll road). The road was originally headquartered on the ranch he established upon arriving in the valley (Negus apparently squatted on the property until formally filing for it in 1879). William's wife, Anna, provided the dinners to the travelers riding her husband's stagecoaches.

Throughout the 1870s and early 1880s, Negus continued to expand his stage and freighting business to include not only Helena and Lincoln, but also Fort Benton, Marysville and the Stemple Pass mining camps. The Canyon Creek Volunteer Fire Department is headquartered on the old Negus place.

The history of Canyon Creek is tied directly to Negus and his son-in-law and partner, Moses Root. When Negus received a government contract to deliver mail in 1871, he located the post office at a nearby cluster of buildings called "Georgetown." Although located on someone else's homestead, Negus renamed the new post office "Canyon Creek." After the homesteaders lost their claim in 1884, Root filed on the property. The present Canyon Creek Store may have been built sometime around 1871. William Negus died from an acute skin disorder in 1888; Root continued to operate his business until about the turn of the century.

The Little Prickly Pear Valley has experienced a rich and exciting history that included mining, agriculture and transportation. Although the valley initially developed as a mining district, it quickly switched to more stable and profitable agricultural pursuits when its residents realized the true value of the land.

Helena was dependent not only the revenues generated by the mines, but also on the produce and cattle grown in the valley. The original road through the valley was important in ensuring that Helena benefitted from Marysville's and Lincoln's good fortunes. Today, the valley retains its agricultural setting, but also includes reminders of its mining heritage in the mangled stream beds, placer tailings and the many historic buildings.

FORESTVALE
CEMETERY

BY KIMBERLY MORRISON

When the Forestvale Cemetery opened its gates in 1890, few Helenans would have predicted that some seventeen years later a local newspaper would be touting the property as "God's Acre"—one of the most beautiful suburban parks in the states. But that is exactly how a Helena Daily Independent article described the cemetery in 1907. On the site of a "barren and treeless desert," an isolated arboretum of flowers, trees and other foliage had sprung to life amidst the prairie grass, prickly pear, and rocks of the west Helena valley.

The Forestvale Cemetery, or the Helena Cemetery as it was known before 1896, was designed and landscaped by civil engineer Harry V. Wheeler in 1890. Prior to the development of Forestvale, Helena's civic leaders had begun searching for another burial site for the city. Helena's population had ballooned from 3,000 to nearly 13,000 residents in less than a decade, and space in the three existing denominational graveyards was rapidly disappearing. Thus, in July 1889, the city purchase 120 acres for $3,500 from the Charles E. Colbert ranch, located two and a half miles northwest of town near the Scratchgravel Hills, and the new non-denominational city cemetery found a home.

After the land transaction was finalized, engineer Wheeler began landscaping the graveyard, planting a variety of trees native to the Pacific Northwest, including weeping birch, catalpa, ash, and native spruce and juniper. A small sunken pond was placed in the center of the cemetery, and a large Gothic-arched stone gateway was erected at the entrance to the main avenue. Concentric boulevards lined by hedges and flowers meandered through Forestvale and were laid out in a pattern typical of suburban garden landscaping in the eastern United States during the late 19th century.

Engineer Wheeler's unique sense of design was influenced by his knowledge of rural and suburban parks in New England, where he was reared and educated, and by his sensitivity to people's apprehension of death and the grave. By landscaping the Forestvale Cemetery as a suburban forest, he and the newly-created Helena Cemetery Association (which had formed in August of 1890 to direct the financial management and to ensure the care of Forestvale) hoped to quiet people's anxieties and provide a peaceful resting place.

With two years, the cemetery had matured and had become more cosmopolitan in nature. Although it at first rejected the burials of non-white and underprivileged people here, the Helena Cemetery Association reversed its policies, allowing some Chinese, African-American, and indigent interments. The remains of eighteen Chinese were removed from town to the new city cemetery by October 1892, and by 1920, approximately 120 people had been buried in "China Row" in the northwest block of the graveyard. Thirty African-Americans were also buried in the cemetery between 1890 and 1956. County commissioners purchased ten acres adjacent to Forestvale at the turn of the 20th century for the county's indigent dead, and the Cemetery Board of Trustees donated an additional parcel of land for indigent burials in 1917.

The simple, yet well kept markers and headstones of Helena's minorities and poor are in stark contrast to the elaborate tombs of some of Montana's most accomplished statesmen and pioneers. Namesakes of many of Helena's streets are etched into the granite and marble sepulchers in Forestvale—names such as Floweree, Ming, Sanders, Hauser, Holter, Ewing, and Kessler. Yet it is the less well known individuals buried here who testify to Montana's colorful residents and rich social history.

Interments include Catherine Sinclaire Sligh, the daughter of a prominent Helena physician and a "wholly unselfish Christian" who died a few weeks before her marriage in 1896; W.L. Peoples, a professional baseball player in Helena between 1900 and 1910; John X. Biedler, a vigilante lawman and "public benefactor" who died in 1890; Annie Kelley, an African-American maid buried within the family plot of her employers, the W.R. Dorsey family; Leigh Miltz Marlow who, legend has it, took a suicidal plunge from a dorm window at the University of Montana in Missoula in 1929; and Lieutenant Eugene S. French, a Spanish-American War veteran and one of 220 veterans who were buried in Forestvale by 1956.

The Forestvale Cemetery experienced severe financial problems during the late 1980s, but it was salvaged by a group of hard-working Helenans who recognized its importance. They raised nearly $55,000 to prevent its abandonment, but it soon became apparent that more funding was needed for future improvements and the perpetual care of Forestvale. A public awareness drive began in early 1991 to inform area residents of the financial straits of the cemetery and the consequences of limited funding if a cemetery district were not created. Consequently during the April election of that year, residents voted to establish a district that guaranteed funding for Forestvale.

The Forestvale Cemetery was listed on the National Register of Historic Places in 1990, recognizing it as a historical site and resting place for 14,280 people, several of whom represent Montana's most industrious families and all of whom paint an accurate portrait of the social and economic stratifications of the Helena community. To stroll through Forestvale today is like walking on the pages of Big Sky history, for both little-known and famous pioneers and their descendants rest in the natural beauty, solitude and sanctity of "God's Acre."

GEORGE LANE/HELENA INDEPENDENT RECORD

Water and Stone: Canyon Ferry Dams

By Chere Jiusto

The Missouri River valley outside of Helena has been a source of electrical power since the late 19th century. Over the years, four dams were constructed near Helena, changing the course of our history and taming the raging waters of the mighty river.

In the late 19th century, electricity was state-of-the-art technology, and demand for electrical power grew, particularly to fuel growing industries. Montana's booming gold, silver and copper mines, smelters and other industrial processing operations drained all the electrical power that early coal-fired generators could produce.

At the same time, emerging towns and cities began to clamor for electricity. Helena was the first city in Montana to electrify, providing many previously unheard-of luxuries to residents of the young city. Electricity was wired into buildings during the 1880s; in 1882, telephone service was connected; and in 1886, electric trolley service began around town.

The First Canyon Ferry Dam

The Canyon Ferry Dam was the brainchild of Samuel T. Hauser, territorial governor and prominent 19th century Montana capitalist. Hauser was one of the first to look to Montana's rivers and see the potential of harnessing water-generated power.

Seeking a source of power for the United Smelting and Refining Company's plant at East Helena, between 1890 and 1892 he first laid plans for a small dam on McClellan Creek in the Elkhorn Mountains southeast of Helena. Forestalled by the national economic Panic of 1893, the McClellan Creek project

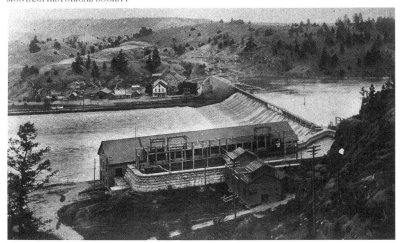

The first Canyon Ferry dam produced hydropower from 1898 until 1950.

was never begun. But shortly thereafter, Hauser turned his sights to bigger water, and to the rugged Missouri River for power source.

Plans for a dam on the Missouri River began with surveys in 1894; in the spring of 1896, the Helena Water and Electrical Power Company was formed with Hauser at the helm. A year later, work crews began dam construction at a site just twenty miles from Helena, where the river narrowed enough to be spanned readily. The new dam would be placed at the mouth of Black Rock Canyon, a site known as Canyon Ferry, and would power the smelter at East Helena. Any leftover juice would be sent to the city of Helena, or on to Corbin for the Peck-Montana Company plant.

Dam crews earned twenty-five cents per hour for their sweat and toil: board and a bunk was seventy-five cents a day in Canyon Ferry. Hugh Cooper, the supervising engineer, was a master dam builder who went on to international fame for his later work, most notably the Dnieprostroy Dam and power plant in Russia, completed in the early 1930s.

As one early journalist noted, in its day the building of the first Canyon Ferry Dam was an engineering feat, "a constant battle with men matching their wits against the strength and

The second Canyon Ferry dam went into operation in 1953.

treachery of an age old river." Freighters hauled stone and timbers in by wagon. Sawn lumber was milled in Bonner, shipped to Townsend by rail, dumped into the river and floated downstream to the dam site.

When finished, the Canyon Ferry Dam stood 29 feet high and 500 feet long, a stalwart stone and timber crib structure. It held back a lake seven miles long and two to three miles wide, which was named Lake Sewell. The powerhouse was also of stone hewn from the nearby hills, and contained ten turbines, each capable of generating 750 kilowatts of electricity.

Power from the Canyon Ferry Dam flowed to the United Smelting and Refining Company plant via a powerline reputed to have been the world's first high-tension transmission line. And there was enough extra current to fulfill the promise, to the wonderment of many that "very soon, the people of Helena will read at night by the aid of electricity generated by water!"

Some of the electricity made its way farther south, funneled from the Missouri River to the mines of Butte. At the time of completion, the Canyon Ferry–Butte powerline gained recognition as the longest and largest hydroelectric powerline in the world.

In 1900, Helena Water and Electric Power Company reorganized as the Missouri River Power Company. Demand for hydro-power was tremendous, and it was reported matter-of-factly that Hauser's new company "accepted business of the kind it prefers," turning down contracts with municipal customers to reserve current for heavy industrial users "such as the smelters and the mines that use current for their blowers or air condensers and their pumps."

The mighty wheels in the Canyon Ferry powerhouse turned for fifty-two years, from April 2, 1898 until, on March 15, 1950, they ground to a halt: "The grandaddy of Montana's electric power industry has accepted retirement after half a century of service...The generators and turbines ground to a quiet stop at noon today."

THE NEW CANYON FERRY DAM

"When the historians come around 85 years from now in the year 2034, they may be looking for evidence of our prowess in the development of natural assets, including large acreages placed under irrigation by the new Canyon Ferry dam.

Canyon Ferry dedication

On July 23, 1949, eighty-five years after gold was discovered in Last Chance Gulch, a dynamite blast reverberated through Helena's Missouri River valley. Shaking the original Canyon Ferry Dam to its foundations, the blast kicked off construction of a new Canyon Ferry Dam, one which would dwarf the old hand-hewn stone dam and sentence it to a watery grave. On hand for four days of dam-christening festivities were several western governors, and Montana's own Gary Cooper and George Montgomery.

By Act of Congress, the new dam was part of the Missouri River Basin project, a grand plan to place a chokehold on the raging Missouri along its entire length, commandeering its waters for irrigation and hydroelectric power, and controlling flooding. Canyon Ferry Dam, a keystone in the upper reaches of this giant Bureau of Reclamation project, was planned to open over 500,000 acres of farmland above Fort Benton to new or improved irrigation.

Similar in design to the Grand Coulee Dam, the new Canyon Ferry Dam was an engineering spectacle. It took four years and crews of up to 500 men to string the enormous concrete apron across the canyon. Towering 172 feet above the riverbed, it was large enough to handle the run-off from over 15,000 square miles of Big Sky country.

Above the dam, Canyon Ferry village cropped up. A cluster of small houses at the head of the reservoir (now used by Canyon Ferry Limnological Institute), it was home to the dam engineers and builders. The heart of the village is the old Canyon Ferry Schoolhouse, built about 1916. While the old ferry landing and townsite lie 170 feet down at the bottom of the lake, the schoolhouse was moved up to the village before the waters rose, and saved.

Progress on the dam was hampered early on by shortages of carpenters and a break in the diversion flume. Throughout 1950, the contractors, Canyon Constructors, rushed to raise the dam walls high enough to contain spring runoff and flooding. Using pioneer ingenuity, an old gold dredge was enlisted to excavate the dam footings, and scoop up gravel for the concrete mix. Waste fly ash from industrial stacks was also added to the recipe, to save money and strengthen the bond.

At the same time, valley residents scrambled to move or salvage family homes, barns, and other buildings. The Cooney family had the distinction of relocating for a second time; their first move was forced by construction of the original Canyon Ferry Dam across the mouth of Black Rock Canyon in 1898.

Racing ahead of the dam builders, archaeologists from the Smithsonian and Montana State University (Missoula), along with historians from the National Park Service and the Montana Historical Society, combed the floodplain to survey the valley's cultural relics. They recorded sites, mines, ghost towns and rock art that told the long story of the Missouri Valley, and its people.

The archaeological team discovered ancient cave and rock shelters, extensive campsites, tipi rings, and petroglyphs from periods when the Blackfeet, Gros Ventre, Shoshone and other Indian people regularly occupied this valley.

The historical crew identified remains of human activity

from more recent times: three camps of the Lewis and Clark expedition, where the door to western expansion was cracked open; Cave Town, Avalanche Creek and other old mining towns, still ringing with the sounds of picks and gold pans from the valley's gold rush days; the Diamond City–Canyon Ferry stage road that wove a loose web along the river corridor, connecting early farms and fledgling towns; and the old rock schoolhouse in Bundy Gulch where children scratched their futures on chalk slates.

The Canton ghost town, about six miles north of Townsend, included a hotel, dance hall, dry goods store, saloon, bunkhouses and a homestead that recalled a bustling past.

"As many as 108 couples at one time [danced] on the floor at Canton...It was a gathering place or community centre for the people of the valley. There they came for letters from their friends back home. There the women bought their groceries and dry goods. On Sundays, the young men gathered to run foot races, to play poker and see horse races. Gambling was wide open everywhere. But horse racing was the favorite sport and Canton held no mean record as a racing center, some of the pony races run on her lane were as good as could have been seen anywhere in the state."

All this and more lay in the path of the new Canyon Ferry reservoir, which swamped twenty-five miles of river bottom, and overran the banks of Lake Sewell, the reservoir created by the first dam. When the spillway gates were shut in September of 1953, 2 million gallons—fifty times more water than Lake Sewell—backed up over the next two years to form Canyon Ferry Lake.

Four more years passed before the irrigation system from Canyon Ferry Dam was finished. In all, the Helena Irrigation Project included a two-and-a-half-mile tunnel snaking under the Spokane Hills, the thirty-two-mile Helena Irrigation Ditch, and Lake Helena regulating reservoir. Finally, on April 1, 1959, the taps were opened and the first water from Canyon Ferry flowed out to irrigate Helena-area farms.

Today, Missouri River waters still flow through the mighty Canyon Ferry Dam, and spill out into the Helena valley, drenching alfalfa and powering computers.

Montana City

❧

BY LEANNE KURTZ

A little east and a little south of the quarries of Last Chance Gulch lies a town whose name connotes prominence and distinction. It is a town whose title reflects the great expectations of its early inhabitants. In 1863, it was a flourishing mining camp with nearly 4,000 residents, and now it is home to hundreds of residents, a cement plant, a school, restaurants, casinos, bars and even a hair styling salon.

Montana City, currently one of the Helena area's fastest-growing "bedroom communities," has endured cycles of boom and bust, depression, a devastating fire and construction of Interstate 15. There have even been rumors of a buried treasure beneath a large granite rock not far from the original townsite. Although nothing of the original burg remains above ground today, Montana City's fifteen minutes of fame and fortune spawned some colorful stories.

White prospectors were certainly not the first to recognize the value of the flat on which Montana City now stands. Native Americans had been camping and quarrying chert in the area for thousands of years, as evidenced by the valley's archaeological record. It was gold, however, that brought the thousands of earnest settlers to the banks of Prickly Pear Creek in the early 1860s.

The first building at the site constructed for winter shelter in 1862 was named Fort Minnesota and, by 1864, several houses had been built with many more in the works. The diggings along the creek were producing some of the largest nuggets in the territory, and the usual businesses attending mining settlements of the West soon began springing up around the dwellings.

One optimistic settler wrote, "From the rapid progress we

are making, there will soon be city here, which, for business, wealth and population may ere long rival Virginia [City] and others of its older sister towns."

Town founders Henry M. Hill and James Gourley, among others, sought to incorporate the settlement during the 1864 territorial legislative session in Bannack. A professionally drawn town plat (complete with ten streets criss-crossing each way just west of Prickly Pear Creek) was presented to the legislature as House Bill 15, "An Act to Incorporate the Town of Montana." House Bill 15 sailed through the process with little difficulty and Montana City was on its way to greatness.

Having suffered such titles as "Pear Town," "Prickly Pear Toll Gate," "Prickly Pear Diggings," and "Prickly Pear Camp," the residents of the newly incorporated city rejoiced at having won such a distinguished designation. Unfortunately, others in the territory (with some political clout) coveted the name, and legislators subsequently gave it to an upstart silver mining town in the Beaverhead Valley. Disappointed citizens of the

Montana City in its second winter, that of 1864.

first Montana City relinquished the name without a fight and officially changed their town to Prickly Pear. It remained so until 1887 when the Postal Service returned the name to its rightful owner.

Prickly Pear saw its heyday in the mid-1860s, supporting thousands of miners, store owners, hotel proprietors and the county government. The town was a mere two-hour horseback ride from Helena and lay directly on the stage route between Fort Benton and Corinne, Utah, a significant shipping corridor. But, as often was the case in mining boom towns, the riches were eventually played out. The growth of business in nearby Helena lured many prospectors away from the dwindling placer mines in Prickly Pear and others joined the rush to Lump, Grizzly and Oro Fino gulches.

In 1903, the *Basin Progress* reported that a devastating fire, supposedly caused by "tramps" on a passing train, destroyed what structures remained of Montana City. Although the occasional prospector continued to dig along the creek, the town had been all but abandoned when the standing timbers fell victim to the fire. The *Progress* tells of a businessman from the East who travelled to Montana in the years following Montana City's demise. He was in search of a location to open a livery stable and upon looking at a map of Montana, saw the name Montana City in big bold letters. After asking around and discovering that no livery stable currently operated in the town, the young entrepreneur believed he had found his niche. The *Progress* recounts that the stranger rented a team from a Helena establishment "keeping the purpose of his mission a secret, in the fear that someone might snatch the prize from his grasp." The clever capitalist was directed to Montana City, but after ranging ten miles from Helena, worried that he had missed the road. "At the McCamley placers," reads the *Progress*, "he found a man, of whom he inquired how much farther it was to Montana City. 'You passed it back on the road there you darned chump,' was the reply and the tenderfoot returned home to reflect that the people of Montana weren't overlooking any really good things on their own account."

One really good thing in Montana City that everyone may be overlooking is a bucket full of buried treasure including "sapphires as large as Weezie bird's eggs" and nuggets of pure gold. The story goes that Patrick O'Malley, an Irish prospector who frequented Montana City's watering holes, boasted regularly of his bucket of buried treasure that would ensure him a happy retirement. He claimed he was not at all concerned about spreading word of his fortune because his "family banshee" had escorted him to America to warn him of impending dangers. O'Malley asserted that his sapphires were "of a deep blue that could only be likened to an Irish sky at midnight," and his gold nuggets were like "drops of Montana sunshine on a soft summer day." His words may have been dismissed as the rantings of an inebriated old man had he not appeared in town on occasion sporting giant blue sapphires and gold nuggets. On the morning after he announced his retirement, the prospector was found dead in front of his cabin with a single bullet hole in his head. No evidence ever surfaced that the treasure was found, and for all anyone knows, it remains entombed beneath a large granite rock just outside Montana City with a banshee or two ensuring its safety.

Perhaps Montana City has had a banshee looking out for it as well. After years of anonymity in the first half of the Twentieth Century, Montana City is again a bustling community. Although the 1903 fire wiped out the remaining vestiges of the mining camp, with a little imagination, the log cabins of Prickly Pear City can probably be spied among the split level homes, beyond the rush of semi trucks on Interstate 15.

Many thanks to the late Helena historian Mauck Brammer, for the extensive writings on Montana City that he left behind.

RIMINI

❦

BY HARRIETT C.
MELOY

Red Mountain, ten miles southwest of Helena, one of the tallest pinnacles in the region, reaches an altitude of over 8,200 feet. It acquired its name from the rosy hue that encircles the peak at sundown. On its lower slopes is a scattering of buildings first named Young Ireland and later dubbed Rimini.

Mining journals inform us that, in 1867, John Caplice made the first discovery of minerals on the mountain. He established a claim he named "Lee Mountain." Caplice was more of a merchandiser than a miner. He later operated stores at Cedar Creek, Philipsburg, Missoula, and "New Chicago" before settling in Butte in 1876.

Looking over Rimini to Red Mountain.

EDWARD REINIG PHOTOGRAPH, MONTANA HISTORICAL SOCIETY

Caplice found gold on the original claim, and silver, but miners in the area pursued lead and zinc more actively, possibly because these minerals were more accessible. Most of the claims were lode mines from 1870 on. Lode names were colorful: the Lee Mountain, Nelly Grant, General Grant, Good Friday, Peerless Jenny, Pauper's Dream, Valley Forge and the American Flag.

Miners attracted to the camp were mostly Irish and so, not unexpectedly, the name given the town was "Young Ireland."

In 1884, the name was changed to "Rimini" by the former Montana territorial governor, J. Schuyler Crosby.

There is an interesting story explaining the name change.

Governor Crosby, the scion of an aristocratic New York family, was a personal friend of President Chester Arthur, who appointed him to Montana's governorship. Arriving in Montana in 1883, Crosby was popular with Republicans but not with the more numerous Democrats, so he stayed only one year. He moved to Washington, D.C. and became the nation's assistant postmaster general.

Before coming to Montana, Crosby was the American consul in Italy. He returned to the United States with a soft spot for Italian theater. One day a talented English actor, Lawrence Barrett, whom Crosby knew, visited him in his office and enthusiastically described a new play in which he was acting titled *Francesca de Rimini.* Barrett and Crosby then put their heads together and decided to name an infant mining camp post office in faraway Montana after the play. The miners accepted the name since they believed Crosby to be Irish, and "Rimini" an Irish name.

Naming a post office in a mining camp without a railroad was slightly premature. What the lively hamlet needed most, besides a railroad, was a hotel. At least 150 miners urgently desired to be housed and fed. In early 1884, The *Helena Herald* reported that "Mr. Larue has a hotel which is full every night" and "James Connelly is building a frame house for a hotel." Jurgens and Price advertised their new Rimini store in the Helena newspaper. No report mentions building bars, but the town boasted at least one. With the arrival of families, a church and school were constructed.

Entrepreneurs followed on the heels of the mine workers bringing with them sophisticated mining equipment and know-how. These adventurers discussed the potential of a rail line for the delivery of ore from the Rimini mines direct to the smelter in East Helena. Among the developers was a prominent national figure, James J. Hill, president of the Great Northern Railway. Hill, one of the first to recognize the worth of Rimini's silver, lead and zinc, founded the Red Mountain Consolidated Mining Company. Following the founding of his company, he hoped to route the Montana Central, a branch of the Great Northern, south to Rimini and then east to the Helena & Livingston Smelting & Reduction Company to process ore from the Rimini mines.

Hill's great friend and associate in Montana was C.A. Broadwater, a leading figure in the territory's transportation endeavors who later became a successful financier after founding the Montana National Bank in Helena in 1882.

Always a canny business man, Broadwater bought property on Ten Mile Creek west of Helena to protect James Hill's expectation of driving a rail line south to Rimini, and to prevent the Northern Pacific from acquiring first transportation rights to the mining camp. However, James Hill was counseled by his financial advisers to end the feud with the Northern

Rimini in 1924.

Pacific. As a result, the Northern Pacific built the Rimini–Red Mountain Route in 1886.

The truce forced Broadwater to make alternative plans for the Ten Mile Creek land, so in 1888 he constructed the elegant Broadwater Hotel and Natatorium, three miles west of Helena, and made it one of the most splendid spas in the West.

Meanwhile Hill's scheme for expansion persisted in Rimini as he planned to bore a tunnel into the mountain and build a concentrating plant near his mining enterprise. He died in 1916 before his vision became a reality. The administrators of his estate were refused permission by the city of Helena to erect a smelting operation close to the mine because of the proximity of the Chessman Reservoir, Helena's water supply. In April 1916, the *Montana Daily Record* reported that the city of Helena had acquired Ten Mile Creek water for $450,000. "The situation is unfortunate as the water is vital for Helena as well as for the mines," noted the report.

Developing mining property on the steep slopes of Red Mountain proved more complicated than Hill and his successors anticipated. Tributaries of Ten Mile Creek flooded the area during the spring rainy season, creating almost insurmountable difficulties. Lack of sufficient funds to keep the mines operating exacerbated the problems.

Census figures compiled from 1890 to 1940 reflect growing disaffection for the area's mining potential: 1890, 282 persons; 1910, 99; 1920, 85; 1930, 66; 1940, 68. The current population figure (1990) for this small unincorporated place is 33. Clearly the number of residents continues to fluctuate downward. The 1990 count was, however, taken in April before the summer dwellers arrived.

Rimini, like many small mining towns, could not be characterized as a big producer over the years; nevertheless, the area most certainly possessed rich deposits of high grade ore. Muriel Wolle, in *Montana Pay Dirt,* reports that $7 million was generated in the region between 1864 and 1928.

Mining continues at Rimini today with more advanced knowledge and equipment available, but tricky questions of water and waste are even more challenging than they were a century ago.

Alhambra Hot Springs

❧

By Harriett C. Meloy

During the 1920s and 1930s, returning Intermountain Union College students looked forward to their traditional fall hot tub parties. The "tub," a fairly good-sized, cement-lined swimming pool, could be reached in about twenty minutes driving south from the Helena college by bus. This reservoir was fed by springs so hot that on nippy October evenings classmates could barely see each other through the thick steam. While relaxing in the warm water, the young men and women sometimes reflected on who discovered the springs and when.

They may have been surprised to know that the story began the same year as the discovery of Last Chance Gulch when, in 1864, a prospector by the name of Wilson R. Redding ceased his futile search for gold in Virginia City and determined to go to Helena and build a store. En route to Last Chance Gulch from Virginia City, he stopped in Jefferson City to buy logs. During several days, while waiting for the wood to be whipsawed, he discovered a quartz mine property at the confluence of Warm Springs Creek and Prickly Pear, which he purchased. Adjacent to the mine were hot springs belonging to Sylvanius Dustin, who held squatters' rights to the gushing waters. Redding offered Dustin $3,000 for the site. Dustin accepted payment and was never heard of again.

Pursuing his revised dream of success, in a land he hoped to call home, Redding began a correspondence with Miss Sarah Furnish, a resident of Virginia City. Sarah was the stepdaughter of Dr. G.W. Stein who, incidentally, was credited by some sources with the founding of Alhambra Hot Springs. In February 1866, Redding wrote to Sarah that they were "about to take the most important step of our life: marriage; it is an event which decides fully our future happiness." He went on to say that he was busy looking into various business ventures and could not set the wedding date. He continued: "I hope to propose a day soon as I fear procrastination might prove detrimental to my interests."

Evidently, the marriage was celebrated that spring because in June the Virginia City *Montana Post,* reported that the young couple entertained "weary travelers" en route from Virginia City to Fort Benton by treating them to a "sumptuous repast" at their hot springs ranch. During the course of the evening the host informed the travelers that "his new bathhouse would be shortly completed."

Sarah Redding proved to be an excellent partner for her new husband. A charming hostess and entertainer, she played the piano for dancing at their ranch resort. During the next decades, the couple became parents of four sons and two daughters, one of whom married the first superintendent of Glacier National Park, W.R. Logan. (Logan Pass was named for the Reddings' son-in-law.)

While improving his Springs property, Redding named the resort. His literary bent suggested a reference from faraway Spain. But, when selecting the title, he may have mistaken the Alhama of Granada with the Alhambra, an ancient Moorish palace and fortress. At Alhama, in southern Spain, baths near the river were 112 degrees and very popular with spring and autumn visitors for their "cures of rheumatism and dyspepsia." Redding hoped to create the same popular destination for his springs.

Wilson and Sarah Redding presided over the charming spa for several years, adding a second story to the hotel, and clearing a larger space for dancing in the dining room. However, in October 1873, a Helena news item announced that Alhambra Hot Springs was to be mortgaged to King and Gillette, owners of the toll road between Clancy and Montana City. One might surmise that the resort was not as lucrative as Redding wished it to be, or that the couple had overspent their capital while improving building and grounds. Possibly the Springs' owner hoped to focus more intensely on his quartz mine, the King

Solomon. Another contemporary news item mentioned that the Springs would be "leased to Niedenhafen," but no report of a sale appeared in Helena newspapers.

Meanwhile, the Reddings continued to supervise the house and baths. Redding hoped for traffic from Helena, but Alhambra went virtually unnoticed by Helena citizens until railway transportation became available between Helena and Clancy in the mid-1880s. In July of 1887 a train-load of sixty Helenans visited the Springs for a weekend. By that time, reported an article in the *Helena Herald,* "Alhambra had undergone important improvements, a new hotel of two floors, with modern appointments....The bathing facilities have been enlarged and improved so much that they now rank among the best in the Territory. There are plunge and swimming baths both for ladies and gentlemen, the bountiful supply of water keeping them constantly overflowing and pure....There is no pleasanter spot anywhere within easy reach of the city and certainly for bathing facilities for Helena's thousands it should have the preference," declared the *Herald's* writer. One wonders if C.A. Broadwater might have considered these words as a challenge to his Broadwater Hotel and Natatorium west of Helena, which would be completed in 1889.

The Alhambra supplied not only recreation, but also health benefits for its escalating number of Helena visitors. In 1887, Percy Kennett, a relative of Samuel Hauser, remarked that his trip to Alhambra left him "much benefitted in health though not fully recovered from rheumatism."

A short decade later, in 1896, the *Helena Herald* described the Springs as a popular place for bicycle enthusiasts who could leave Helena early in the morning and arrive at Clancy in time for breakfast.

A rumor circulated in the *Clancy Miner* in 1896 that the Great Northern Railway Company was to purchase the hot springs and surrounding property to build a great natatorium and summer hotel on the grounds. Further mention of the railway company's plans does not appear in subsequent issues of the Clancy newspaper. But in the summer of 1897 when the prominent Dr. and Mrs. Hunter operated the hotel, cottages and swimming pool, additional construction did occur. Perhaps the stately hotel, seen in the accompanying photo, was built at this time; further research may disclose that the Great Northern and Dr. Hunter collaborated on improving the summer recreation spot. Or perhaps the elegant structure might have been built by Mike Sullivan, who owned the Alhambra from the late 1920s through the 1930s.

Hotel at Alhambra Hot Springs, date unknown.

During all those years, despite the resort's changing of hands, Wilson Redding remained a frequent visitor at the resort. He shuffled cards in the recreation room and waited for other poker players to take a hand. No doubt his mind noted with pleasure the changes the years had brought to this spot. Both Sarah Redding and Wilson died in Jefferson County not far from Alhambra Hot Springs; Sarah in 1912 and Wilson in 1930 at the age of ninety-one.

In 1959, a sudden fire destroyed the resort, with a resulting loss of $100,000 due to damage of buildings and grounds. The owner was W.L. Bompart of Helena, who had just bought the property from Dr. R.G. Bayles of Bozeman. Bompart was spending $25,000 on improvements at the time of the fire.

The Hillbrook Nursing Home occupies the site at this time.

BUILDINGS

Signs of the Times

BY CHERE JIUSTO

Since the first enterprising merchant rolled into the Last Chance mining camp to hawk his wares, signs have been a prominent part of Helena's scenery. In the Queen City, where the new mixes freely with the old, ghosts of historic hand-painted signs are reminders of a past gone by, of businesses and products now extinct.

Today in Helena, just a dozen or so of these treasures remain.

Over the years, most of the hand-painted signs have been lost to time and newer modes of advertisement. Yet on Breckenridge and Rodney, the old THOMAS SILLER'S LIVERY signs echo a vanished way of life, advertising feed, sales and boarding stables. Around the corner, "CAPITAL CRACKER" and "REX, THE PERFECT SODA CRACKER" from Helena's National Biscuit Company would still taste good with a glass of milk.

Meanwhile downtown, both sides of the Iron Front Hotel declare "Eddy's BREAD good... to eat!" Over on the Parchen Building, the "GENERAL ARTHUR CIGAR" is guaranteed to "SUIT ALL MANKIND." Down in the 400 Block of the Gulch, PALMQUIST ELECTRIC and HUBER•JASMIN•OTT BLACKSMITHING are still with us.

And day after day, above the heads of bustling downtown office workers and shoppers, Helena Hardware's "WORLD FAMOUS" Sherwin Williams paint still spills out to "COVER THE EARTH" from "AFRICA" to "EUROPE."

Advertising signs in America were inspired by predecessors in Europe, where the earliest commercial signs were often simple symbols for the goods and trades offered. For a public that was largely illiterate, a sheep for a tailor, the apothecary's mortar and pestle, or a foaming ale tankard on the local pub declared to all passers-by the nature of the business. Some symbols were more cryptic, like the three balls for a pawnbroker, which derived from the coat of arms of the powerful Medicis, a banking family in medieval Italy.

Many signs hung from buildings, above streets and walkways. These eye-catching signs were probably effective advertisements, but they proved to be hazardous at times. In En-

Parchen and Paynter's City Drug Store was a sampler of the sign-painter's art.

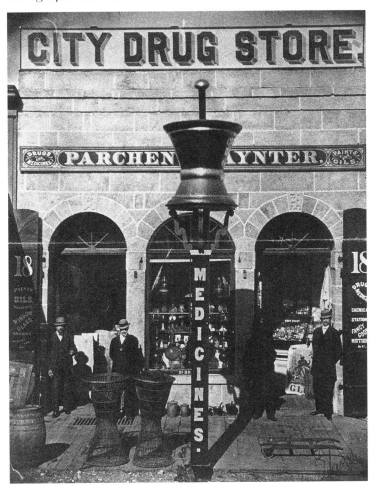

gland people complained. "The creaking signs not only kept the citizens awake at night, but they knocked them off their horses, and occasionally fell on them too." By the end of the 18th century, the British had outlawed many projecting signs, in favor of flat signs mounted flush to the buildings.

In America, projecting signs, hanging signs and those fixed to buildings were all commonplace. In Helena, it was no different. Old photographs of the Gulch reveal a cacophony of signs, all trumpeting the wares and services of the shops to which they were attached. Early on, the big black boot of Gurney the shoemaker swung out over the Gulch along with other signs of the times—a diamond ring above a jewelry shop, a big tooth for the dentist. These symbolic signs became landmarks known to all, including miners who did not read, and the numerous immigrants in the mining camp who spoke and read little or no English.

As the 19th century wore on, signs often became incorporated into the design of new buildings. Sign bands just above storefronts and large inset panels on building fronts were used to display signs, while big blank walls on the sides and backs of buildings became favorite sites for large painted signs.

Hand-painted signs were an art form in themselves, designed and executed by professional sign companies. Some artisans made sign painting a way of life—have paintbrush, will travel—journeying from town to town painting new signs and touching up old signs as they weathered and faded. Blocky black and white lettering, splashed with green, red, blue and yellow were favorites from the painter's palette.

Tarnished jewels gleaming in back alleys and side streets, these old signs grow more rare and precious by the year. Clinging valiantly to old brick, they flake a little more with each changing season.

Like all of us, they grow older: their voices, once brash, are now softer; their colors, once loud, are now muted. Yet the lines and the cracks, the peeling and fading breathes into them a beauty that grows by the year. It's the kind of beauty gained by turning one's face to the sun and the clouds, to the wind and the rain.

Ghost Story Mystery

BY JON AXLINE

He who does not fill his world with phantoms remains alone.

Antonio Porchia, 1968

Helenans live among ghosts. The old buildings we live in and among are ghosts of an earlier time. Through them, we can readily discern the popular architectural styles of times past; they also bear the marks of long-dead builders and, oftentimes, the decorative flourishes of people from another era. According to some, the spirits of the original owners also remain behind to complete the illusion and, sometimes affect the current owners in more intangible ways. The following is a "true" ghost story that was reported to the author by a woman who will be referred to as "Sharon." The house on "Center Street" still stands and appears much as it did when the subject of this story was alive.

The American Heritage Dictionary defines a ghost as "The spirit or shade of a dead person, supposed to haunt living persons or former habitats." Some specters appear corporeal, while others seem luminous, transparent or ill-defined. Ghosts move through solid matter, appear and disappear abruptly, and are always clothed. Importantly, for this story, ghosts appear in clothing that was popular at the time they died. This haunting contains all the classic elements that involve most ghostly visitations. It concerns a benevolent lost soul that does not realize it's dead and only wants to rejoin its parents. Fortunately, the historical record can provide some additional information that,

The house on "Center Street."

pardon the pun, fleshes out Sharon's account of the apparition's tragic sojourn on Center Street.

The ghost's name was Margaret and she had curly brunette hair and wore a Victorian-style dress; she appeared to be about four years old. According to Sharon, Margaret "missed the people who loved her, held her and rocked her"; unfortunately, she had to stay in the house and wait for her family to come and get her. If the written record is correct, Margaret had been waiting for her family for a very long time.

Sharon first became aware of the little girl's presence shortly after moving into the two story house in the early 1970s. Sometimes she heard laughing and playing upstairs. Occasionally, her two-and-a-half-year-old daughter would play with the ghost, accepting her as just another playmate. Even Sharon's infant son saw Margaret and was not bothered by her appearance. Sharon later wrote that from one room came "sounds of a little girl cooing, talking and babbling as to her dolls...By the window at the south end of the hall came the sound of a rocking chair. A real rocking chair placed there rocked itself and would obviously stop when someone took conscious note of it."

Early one morning, Sharon became aware of an unseen presence standing next to her bed. When she opened her eyes, the phantom faded away. From then on, however, the little ghost would regularly appear by her bed and sob quietly about her lost parents. At that point, Sharon seemed to have gained the trust of the shade and the two somehow formed a psychic connection. She would "see things [Margaret] had seen and felt, such as watching a black surrey driving out where Lake Helena is now. The most traumatic was a man in a checkered suit with black hair and a mustache, and a woman whose dark silk skirts were large and suffocating, forcibly taking little Margaret from the house." What was obvious to Sharon was that the ghost was very sad, lonely and confused; she desperately wanted her parents.

Sharon often saw Margaret standing near the north bedroom window, crying into a handkerchief as she looked forlornly toward the old Canyon Ferry Road. In the winter, there was a round circle melted into the frost on the window as "when a child breathes on a frosted window." At least two other people saw her standing at the window over the next three years.

Finally, however, it came time for Sharon to move. Because Margaret had become part of the family, she asked the apparition to move across the street with them. Margaret refused and remained in the house, patiently awaiting her parents' return. Eventually, Sharon and her friends took pity on Margaret and told her it was time to join her parents. The impromptu exorcism appeared to have been successful and little Margaret joined her mother and father on the Other Side.

Although a firm believer in the "spirit" of places (this doesn't necessarily mean possession by spirits; it's just a feeling for the people and events of the place), there was a need on my part to find some hard evidence for Sharon's story or be able to place it in some kind of historical context. Luckily, the history of the house and its former owners is well-documented in the public record.

The property was originally purchased by a Midwest mining speculator named Moses Manuel and his wife, Josephine, sometime after they arrived in Helena in 1881. By 1887, the Manuels had leased the lots to William and Anna Zastrow, who built the existing house in late 1887 or 1888. The Gothic Revival-style was a popular architectural style in Helena from the late 1860s until the 1890s. William also came to Helena in 1881 and, apparently, knew Moses through their affiliation with the Ancient Order of United Workmen, a fraternal society with headquarters at the Parchen Block on Broadway. A native of Germany, William was employed as a carpenter, bookkeeper and real estate agent between 1881 and 1912. The 1900 census shows only William and Anna living in the house, although they occasionally took in borders during the 1890s. In April,

1904, Anna died at age forty-nine. William married Marie Hauser the following year. William died in the house following a brief illness the day after the *Titanic* sank in April 1912. Marie continued to live in the house until she transferred ownership of it to her sisters in October 1927; she died in February 1933.

Based on the information collected from the historical record, little Margaret may have been the daughter of William and Anna Zastrow. She was clearly not related to the Manuels, who lived two blocks from the Zastrows. When Moses died in a mining accident near Corbin in July 1905, his fraternity brother, William Zastrow, brought the body back to Helena. Upon his death, Moses left behind his wife and three adult children. There is no evidence indicating that the Manuels ever lived in the house.

Because of her Victorian-style dress, it seems likely Margaret died sometime between 1888 and 1900. There is no mention of any children in Anna's or William's obituaries, nor does Margaret appear in the census. It is not currently known when she died, what killed her or where she is buried. If Margaret was truly William and Anna's daughter, she was probably their only child. By 1900, Anna was too old to bear children and Marie was nearing the end of her child-bearing years when she married William in 1905.

Both William and Anna, along with Marie, were interred at Forestvale Cemetery. The first burials there date to 1890 when the cemetery was established. There is no record of Margaret's burial at Forestvale. If she died before 1890, it seems likely she would have been buried at Benton Avenue Cemetery or the old Catholic cemetery east of town. Unfortunately the records for the Benton Avenue Cemetery are incomplete with many unmarked graves and headstones that have lost their inscriptions; the fate of the Catholic cemetery is another story…

Although the historical record provides a framework for the possibility of Margaret's post-death presence in the Center Street house, it does not divulge any information about the little girl herself. Maybe something will come to light later, but for now it remains a mystery. Maybe there is more than a little truth to Shakespeare's statement in Hamlet, "There are more things in heaven and earth, Horatio, than are dreamt of in your philosophy."

East Helena Smelter

BY LEANNE KURTZ

Imagine a mountain lake shimmering in the summer sun, kids playing in the water, people fishing and lazing about in boats and on the shore. This could be just about any recreation area in Montana. But something is different about this lake. It sits in the shadow of four towering smokestacks. This lake is the East Helena smelter lake, and from its origins shortly after construction of the smelting plant in 1888, it afforded residents of Helena and its sister to the east prime recreational opportunities. These days, the lake is no longer present (and if it was, would likely not be crowded with recreation enthusiasts!), but the smelter and its smokestacks are a long-standing landmark in the Helena Valley and have played an integral part in the development of the community in which it resides.

Montana is well-known for its mining history. Indeed, mining was the reason white settlers first came to the region. With the growth of the industry, and the advancements of mining technology, it became profitable to extract minerals from large amounts of hard rock (lode mining) in addition to gathering free minerals from streams (placer mining). Since no smelters yet existed in Montana, early lode miners shipped huge amounts of ore elsewhere for refining. Wickes, a small settlement twenty-five miles south of Helena, became the site of one of the first ore processing smelters in then Montana Territory. Helena was too rich in minerals, however, to make practical shipping ore elsewhere, even twenty-five miles, for processing. East Helena, then known as Prickly Pear Junction, seemed to have many features that made it a desirable smelting location. Rail lines had recently been constructed, and water and limestone were readily available.

In 1888, the Helena & Livingston Smelting and Refining Company purchased land in present-day East Helena for the purposes of constructing a smelter. That same year, portions of the facility at Wickes were moved to the site, in addition to trained Wickes smelter employees. The plant began operating in 1889, funded partially by Helena residents who contributed $250,000 of the $1 million eventually collected for start-up and operation. The *Helena Weekly Independent* of May 28, 1889 reported that three stacks were operable, each with a capacity of processing seventy tons of ore every twenty-four hours. Soon, the paper stated, a fourth stack would be added, allowing the plant to process 200 tons of ore per day.

Out-of-state interests had been intimately involved in the funding and completion of the smelting plant, and in 1899 the American Smelting and Refining Company (ASARCO) was established in New Jersey to oversee management of sixteen smelters, eighteen refineries and several mines throughout the United States. ASARCO acquired the East Helena plant shortly after the company's organization.

Directly at the heels of opening day at the smelter in East Helena arrived numerous businesses where plant employees could unload their wages on necessities (food, lumber, and blacksmith services) and frivolities (ice cream, booze, and a haircut). In addition to the stores and services offered, East Helena was able to support two newspapers near the turn of the century, the *Record* and the *Republican*. It was near this time, however, that the thriving businesses in East Helena began to falter, as the streetcar tracks were extended from Helena, allowing easy transportation to shopping and other opportunities in the booming metropolis of Helena a few miles west.

From its first days of operation, ASARCO *was* East Helena. The company provided the livelihood for nearly all of the town's residents and sponsored numerous educational, civic and recreational endeavors. In addition to the smelter lake, which also provided a decent spot for ice skating in the winter, ASARCO sponsored a community band, equipping musicians with instruments and uniforms. East Helena also had its own company-sponsored baseball team that, from the sounds of it, would have given even a professional team a run for its money.

In the early days, the East Helena smelter provided the community's lifeblood at work, and also all sorts of recreational opportunities.

Company employees could not have been at a loss for things to do on their off-hours. In addition to the band, baseball games and water sports, ASARCO constructed tennis courts and a nine-hole golf course for the use of its hard-working employees. Although not as diverse or populated as the company towns of Butte and Anaconda of that era, East Helena certainly had its share of international flavor. Eastern and central Europeans populated the town, so much so that the company posted signs for employees in Austrian and Polish as well as English. In the early 1920s, ASARCO began publication of a monthly newsletter, the *Crucible.* The newsletter's primary purpose was to promote safety among the plant employees, but also reported items of employee interest such as marriages, births, deaths and social activities.

Although the extent to which exposure to lead was harmful was not known in the detail to which it is understood today, measures were taken to reduce the contact plant employees had with the by-products of the smelting process. Great pride was taken in the giant fans that blew the smoke and smelter wastes out of the buildings plant workers occupied. Since that time, concern for the air, water, and land affected by lead smelting operations has generated intense controversy and prompted the implementation of regulations unheard of at the turn of the century.

The East Helena smelter has certainly witnessed extensive change in the Helena Valley over the last 100 years, not only in appearance, but also in the attitudes and social organization of the people who work in its buildings and live in its shadow. Ease of transportation to Helena has negated the need for sponsorship of recreational and social programs. No longer strictly a plant town, East Helena has become more of a Helena suburb, supporting an ever-growing number of subdivision developments. Consider the metamorphoses these stacks have seen in their lifespan the next time the slag piles play host to the annual Fourth of July fireworks display, or as you drive past the columns at night, illuminated by the brightly flashing lights warding off unwary airplane pilots and migrating waterfowl.

The Empire Mine and Mill

By Jon Axline

When dinosaurs ruled the earth about 70 to 80 million years ago, the formation of the Rocky Mountains caused the creation of a colossal geological intrusion called the Boulder Batholith. The feature was (and continues to be) important to Montana's development. Essentially a semi-subterranean granite mountain, the batholith is a virtual treasure trove of precious metals, including copper, lead, silver and, most importantly for this chapter, gold. The mining camps of Butte, Elkhorn, Diamond City, Helena and Marysville are located on the batholith where it pierces the earth's surface. The Empire Mine is located on the Boulder Batholith and consists of a rich lode-bearing vein about twenty feet wide and over a mile long. The mine had a profound impact on the Marysville Mining District.

Although hard rock mining began in the Helena area in 1864, it was not until the mid-1870s that the Marysville area recorded its first lode claim when Nate Vestal located the Penobscot Mine in 1873. Two years later, Tommy Cruse filed a claim on Bald Mountain and soon followed it with the discovery of the district's centerpiece—the famous Drumlummon Mine. From Marysville, prospectors scoured the surrounding mountains in search of other El Dorados. By 1880, the mountains around Mount Belmont were marked by small—but mostly profitable—hard rock mines. There were 338 mines operating in Lewis and Clark County by 1884—most were in the Marysville area.

One of these, the Empire Mine, was located about three miles from Marysville high up on the west face of Mount Belmont on Lost Horse Gulch. The mine consisted of three major quartz veins, including the Empire Lode, and fifteen smaller veins. The gold quartz was extracted through three shafts, the largest of which was 2,300 feet long and about 400 feet deep. Through interconnecting tunnels, the Empire shafts were linked with two other mines, the Whippoorwill and the Smithville. The richest ore in the Empire was located between the surface and the 300-foot level.

The Empire Mine was established by John Stemple in January 1881, and the claim patented two years later. Stemple's operation was simple and included only a stone ore crusher, called an arrastra, to process the ore. Helena entrepreneur Thomas Hickey and a partner named Cotter purchased the mine from Stemple in late 1883. When acquired by the partners, the ore was rumored to be worth $172 a ton, making it a most profitable venture for the would-be tycoons. They immediately expanded Stemple's workings by sinking two more shafts and constructing a small stamp mill. In 1885, M.A. Leeson reported that the "wonderful richness of this lead, [has] required additional machinery for the manipulation of this vast body of ore...." Helena mining engineer F.L. Sizer's description of the operation was somewhat less effusive than Leeson's. He stated that the mine "was little more than a prospect, opened by cuts and shallow shafts, none of them over seventy feet deep." In late 1885, Hickey and Cotter doubled the size of their stamp mill and placed the operation on the market. Because of the high concentrations of gold and silver ore and its accessibility, the partners easily attracted the interest of outside investors in their enterprise.

In 1886, a British conglomerate purchased the Empire Mine and operated it under the aegis of the Golden Leaf Corporation, Ltd. (the nearby Drumlummon Mine was also owned by British businessmen, many of whom also owned stock in the Empire Mine). With Helena serving as the principal supply point, the company immediately began expanding the mine.

By 1888, the Empire mill could process 250 tons of ore per day.

One of their first accomplishments was the construction of a telephone line between Marysville and the Empire. The mine's camp was served by a daily stage from Marysville. Sometimes, however, if the coach was overloaded, the passengers were obliged to walk up the steep grade to the camp.

Shortly after purchasing the mine, the British company ordered the construction of a sixty-stamp mill and amalgamation plant to process the ore on the hillside a half-mile below the mine adit. A 1932 report described the mill as "splendidly constructed [of] masonry retaining walls, while the framework of the structure itself consists of Douglas-fir from the Pacific Coast with all timbers throughout the mill dapped and bolted." When completed in January 1888, the mill could process 250 tons of ore a day fed by gravity from 4,000-ton–capacity storage bins to the processor. With the addition of foreign capital and construction of the mill, the mine became enormously profitable and paid out $250,000 in dividends to its stock-holders in 1888. In 1890, the Empire Mine produced $3 million in gold and employed sixty men. The operation was managed by J.H. Longmaid and an assistant, Henry Northey. The mine and mill continued to thrive until 1893 when it fell prey to internal strife between the controlling and minority stockholders of the company. It is not clear what caused the problem, but economic panic generated by the closure of British silver mints in India certainly had an impact on the mine's fortunes. From 1893 to 1900, the mine was operated only sporadically by various lessees.

In 1900, Owen Byrnes organized the Empire Syndicate and leased the mining property from the British company's shareholders. An engineer with roots in the Butte mines, Byrnes had come to Lewis and Clark County in 1888. After working in several mines around Marysville, he turned his attention to resurrecting the Empire Mine and one of its neighbors, the M. K. Mine. Shortly after leasing the Empire operation, Byrnes hired fifteen men to pump water out of the mine and build a small cyanide plant near the tailings dump. The plant reprocessed 3,000 tons of tailings, recovering $14,000 in gold between 1900 and 1903. The company's efforts were hampered by the substantial amount of copper in the tailings, which rendered the amalgamation process difficult. Although the syndicate made regular shipments of ore out of the complex, it apparently did not use the stamps within the mill; they were removed and sold in 1917.

Byrnes terminated his agreement with the mine's owners in 1929. Within a few weeks, however, it was leased by the Metalsmith Mine Corporation. The company had great plans for the Empire Mine and Mill complex. It placed a new corrugated metal roof on the mill, extended power lines from Marysville to provide electricity to the property and installed an extensive underground pipe system to supply water to the mill and outbuildings. Nearby springs fed water into a 5,000-gallon storage area located near the complex. From there, the water was pumped through six-inch pipes to all the major buildings on the site; in case of fire, hydrants were also included in the system. A second 5,000-gallon water storage area received water directly from the Empire, Whippoorwill and Smithville mines.

Other buildings at the mine included a well-equipped blacksmith shop and a change house (with showers) near the adit. The company's managers believed the existing buildings on the property could be rehabilitated to accommodate forty to sixty workers at the mine. The company also converted the old stamp mill into a cyanide flotation plant for processing the gold and silver ore.

The 1929 stock market crash and subsequent economic depression ended the Metalsmith company's grandiose plans for reactivating the Empire Mine and Mill. By 1931, they had "liquidated all their debts and forfeited their claims back to the estates from which they leased." It is unclear whether the company ever extracted any ore from the mine or actively utilized the mill.

In 1932, W.M. Manning obtained a new lease on the property and formed Empire Gold Mines to pick up where the previous company had left off. Although Manning intended to take advantage of the improvements made on the property by the Metalsmith company and also announced plans to construct an electric tram between the mine and the mill, he was forced to suspend operations by 1935. Two years later, in 1937, yet another company, the Rex Mining Company, was formed to extract gold from the Empire Mine complex. Headquartered in Helena and Marysville, it offered 1,500,000 shares to investors at ten cents per share. By 1940, however, the company had sold only 6,950 shares in the mine. Despite this, the company employed twenty men and mined forty tons of ore a day. In 1938 and 1939, the company extracted $162,000 in gold before the U.S. government closed it down because of restrictions during World War II. It never reopened.

It is not exactly clear how much gold the mine produced during the years it was in operation. Between 1887 and 1893, however, the mine yielded roughly $6 million to its owners. Lewis and Clark County was one of the leading producers of gold and silver in the state between 1876 and 1893. The Empire Mine was an important component in the network of mines and mills that contributed to the state's economic prosperity during the last century. Its smaller role as a gold mine in the 20th century also reflects the economic patterns that have characterized this century and how gold and silver were secondary to more important metals like copper, zinc and chromium. In recent years, however, the Empire Mine and Mill's value has been its role as an example of Montana's historic mining heritage. The mill's destruction by fire in 1995 severed an important and irreplaceable link to Montana's past.

Events

Naming Helena

⚜

By Vivian A. Paladin

A little over three months after four down-on-their luck prospectors struck it rich in what they called Last Chance Gulch, a meeting was called to organize the mining district, elect officers, authorize the laying out of lots, and give the camp a name.

On October 30, 1864, a group of men, variously reported to number from a dozen to well over thirty, crowded into the cabin of George J. Wood on South Main to begin deliberations. No record was kept of all those present, but it is known that two of the discoverers, John Cowan of Georgia and Reginald (Bob) Stanley of Nuneaton, England, were there. As he did often in the years that followed, the highly literate Stanley provides us with some of the most colorful descriptions of what happened at this historic town meeting.

Yet another notable informant on the matter of naming the future capital of Montana turned out to be a miner named Thomas E. Cooper of Grafton, Dakota Territory, who was elected secretary of the meeting. While the facts were still in his memory, Cooper wrote a letter to his wife, heading it with these words: "Helena, Jefferson County, Montana Territory, Nov. 12, 1864."

"You will see by the heading of this letter that we have given this place a new name," he began. "A few days ago a man wearing the title of Captain Wood called a meeting at his cabin for the purpose of an organization." After confiding that Captain Wood seemed to be seeking some political favors for himself and his father-in-law when he called the meeting at his cabin, Cooper went on to say that John Summerville, not Wood, was elected chairman and "your husband, secretary." He described Summerville, whose name was spelled in various ways in a number of sources, as a very tall man who "seemed even taller in the cabins." He was from Scott County, Minnesota, and at one time had worked as a ship's carpenter in Quebec, Canada. He was also, Summerville wrote, known as a Unionist.

A number of names were suggested for the town, including such facetious old reliables as Pumpkinville and Squashtown. Cooper told his wife he suggested Rochester and C.L. Cutler wanted to call it Winona. There were many more names bandied about, including Tomah, said to be the name of an Indian chief who had frequently watched the first prospectors at work in the gulch.

Finally, according to Cooper, Chairman Summerville rose to his full height as he stood on a pine block and said, "Gentlemen, I see you are not likely to agree upon a name for this place. I propose to call it Helena."

At this juncture, Cooper wrote, "I looked up into his honest face and said, 'Why, Mr. Chairman, do you propose to name this place in honor of the rebel city in Arkansas?' to which he replied, with all the emphasis in his power, 'Not by a d—d sight, sir. I propose to call it Helena in honor of Helena, in Scott County, Minnesota, the best county in the state and the best state in the union!' And with Mr. Summerville's inspiring words the vote was unanimous and I had the honor of recording the name..."

Through the years, the naming of the town gave way to other concerns, but occasionally there were suggestions that the city had been named for popular young women who had lived here in the early years. In its issue of February 13, 1892, the *Helena Herald,* apparently in an effort to set the record straight, published an article headlined "Christening of Helena."

The item began by quoting a letter the publishing Fisk brothers had just received from one Harry Morris of Missoula. "I drop you a few lines to ask you who the city of Helena was named after," the letter began. "There is a bet here in Missoula between myself and another man. He says it was named after Helena P. Clarke and I say it was named after Helena G. Goldberg. Now the bet is at a standstill until we hear from you..."

Before printing an account of what happened at the 1864 meeting, the newspaper began its 1892 story with these words: "There being a great diversity of opinion among new-comers concerning the origin of the name of Helena, in answer to the above the *Herald* now, for the second or third time, prints the record of the proceedings of the meeting held in Last Chance Gulch, which ought to settle the matter."

The minutes said that G.J. Wood, in whose cabin the meeting was held, was elected chairman and T.E. Cooper, secretary. Cooper later wrote a strong letter to the Society of Montana Pioneers challenging the statement that Wood was elected chairman. "This was a great wrong committed by some person," he wrote, "and it is quite time that it was corrected." He wanted the record to show that it was John Summerville, not Wood, who chaired Helena's first town meeting.

Actually, the naming of the town was given short shrift in the official minutes: "After several motions and balloting the name of Helena was given to the town, and G.J. Wood, H. Bruce and C.L. Cutler were elected town commissioners and ordered to lay out the town and get their pay for the work by recording the lots at $2 each..."

In order to further assure its correspondent from Missoula that Helena was not named for any young lady who had ever lived here, the *Herald* in its 1892 article republished a letter it had received ten years earlier from Reginald Stanley. Stanley corroborated much of what Secretary Cooper had reported to his wife, but, predictably, added some color of his own.

"I well remember the night we assembled in Mr. Wood's cabin to give our embryo town a name," he wrote. "Not much time was wasted in talk and not very long speeches were made." Stanley reported, however, that the vote was close between Tomah and Helena, and admitted with some regret that he voted for the Indian name in spite of doubts he had about its origins because he knew there was another town of some importance named Helena.

He was referring to the historic Mississippi River port city of Helena, Arkansas, incorporated in 1833 and the site of a bloody Civil War battle on July 4, 1865. It is still one of Arkansas' most colorful cities, proud of its heritage, its stately mansions and its ranking today as the fourth most important port on the Mississippi.

Stanley was decidedly not referring to the village in Minnesota so dear to the heart of Chairman Summerville. This town, settled in the early 1850s a few miles south and west of Minneapolis by German immigrants, no longer appears on modern maps as a town or city.

But a quick survey using a modern atlas and talking by phone with a number of city and town officials reveals that besides Helena in Arkansas and Montana's capital city, there are four more Helenas in the United States—in Alabama, Georgia, Oklahoma and California. The latter, once a gold camp like Last Chance Gulch, is in the Trinity River country of northwestern California, but is now considered a ghost town.

Helena, Alabama, in the central part of the state, today is a peaceful quiet town of 6,000.

Helena, Georgia, located fifty miles south of Macon in the

These cabins on Jackson Street (with Lawrence at the left) were built in 1867, and are similar to George Wood's cabin on South Main where early residents decided on a name for Helena.

south central part of the state, was once served by two railroads to transport its agricultural products, chiefly cotton.

The Oklahoma town named Helena was founded in 1907 and was once part of the famed Cherokee Strip in north central Oklahoma. It was named for the first postmaster's daughter, and today has a population of 1,100.

Conversations with residents of the towns or their vicinities made it clear that all of them pronounce the name of their town with accent on the second "e"—HelEEna. Research clearly indicates that Montana's future capital city, on the day it was christened in 1864, was also pronounced that way and so was Chairman Summerville's hometown in Minnesota.

Supposition about the reason for the change and when it took place remains supposition to this day. A newspaper clipping dated December 1898, on file at the Montana Historical Society, is headed, "How Helena Got Her Name" and relates a "curious incident" which may have contributed to the change. "There was a fellow here who ran a hack about town, who had painted in big letters on it 'Hellena.' It was only a miss-spelled word, but was naturally pronounced with the accent on the first syllable and gradually during the year and a half that the hack ran in the camp, it became a habit..."

Even Reginald Stanley, writing from his home in 1906, recalled how surprised he was when he visited his "old stamping grounds" in 1882 to find that the town christened Heleena was now pronounced Hellena.

Stanley's description of that christening, republished in 1892, is of even more help in explaining the meaning of the name Helena and why, in this case, there was no intent to honor a known person, including Miss Clarke or Miss Goldberg. John Summerville, Stanley said in his letter to the *Herald,* was tall and jovial, his hair grizzled with years, and must, by 1882, "have gone to that land from whose bourne no traveler returns."

"Among other things," Stanley wrote, "he [Summerville] sedately informed us that Helena was a word of Greek derivation, and, confirming Mr. Woods' recollection, signified 'a town in the interior.' I knew just enough of Greek to have serious doubts about this interpretation, but did not feel sure enough to mention a contradiction, even had I felt so inclined. Had any member been ready to enlighten the meeting with the true facts of the case, that Helena in fabulous history was said to have been the most beautiful woman of her age, and sprung from one of the eggs that Leda, the wife of King Tyndareus, metamorphosed into a goose, brought forth after her amour with Jupiter [Zeus], who took the shape of a swan, I have no doubt the name would have carried by acclimation..."

It seems doubtful that enough of the miners crowded into Captain Wood's cabin in 1864 knew enough about Greek mythology to recognize that they were naming their camp after the most beautiful woman of the ancient world. It is possible, however, that this bizarre legend not only inspired the following bit of doggerel, published in the April 1889 *Helena Board of Trade Journal,* but also suggests why we pronounce the name of our city the way we do.

> *Helena, after a darling, dizzy dame*
> *Of much beauty but spotted fame;*
> *In pronouncing the name*
> *Understand me well,*
> *Strong emphasis should be laid on Hel.*

THE SINGULAR
VOYAGE OF THE
STEAMBOAT *FERN*

BY ELLEN BAUMLER

The year was 1887 and Dr. A.L. Davison, a Twin Bridges physician, was about to embark on an adventure. With much the same spirit that must have sparked the imaginations of Lewis and Clark on their quest, Dr. Davison hoped to prove steamboat navigability of the Missouri River between Townsend and Great Falls. Such a link would provide a pleasant alternative to uncomfortable stage travel and make the ever-present rumors of railroad expansion locally unimportant.

Helenans had long applauded the idea of a steamboat line on the upper Missouri. In 1878, a group of enthusiasts formed the Montana Steam Navigation Company to investigate the likelihood of such an enterprise. Among these would-be river entrepreneurs were Colonel W.F. Wheeler, C.W. Cannon, John Murphy and at least several riverboat captains of some reputation. The party left on September 5, 1878, in several small skiffs from Stubbs' Ferry; their destination was Fort Benton. They recorded "...beautiful, unique and grotesque scenery unequaled and unknown to any other navigable river." That is, they saw firsthand the wonders Helenans still cherish: the Gates of the Mountains. The trip progressed without a hitch and the Company predicted that "...hereafter thousands will follow in our wake and...have as pleasant a voyage."

Progress in procuring steam travel was slow, and so it was with great eagerness that Helenans monitored the building of the first steamship destined for the upper Missouri years later. The Helena spokesperson for the project was Colonel W.F.

Wheeler, who assumed the title of "commodore" during the course of the endeavor. After a trip in May of 1886 to Twin Bridges, where the *Fern* was being built by Dr. Davison and his two sons, Wheeler reported that the boat was coming along nicely and did not "leak a drop." Her capacity would be 75 tons of freight and 100 passengers. Nine thousand feet of cedar went into her construction. Her substantial proportions seemed all the more impressive as she temporarily rested in the shallow waters of the Beaverhead.

After finishing the first construction phase, Davison began to float the *Fern* down the Beaverhead and the Jefferson to the Missouri and Townsend, where she would await her innards: a boiler, two 25-horsepower engines and transmission gears. However, as the *Fern* floated toward her appointed Townsend mooring, her competition was also making a debut.

The *Rose of Helena*, a small steamer manufactured in Dubuque, Iowa, and owned by Judge Nicholas Hilger, arrived in Townsend via the Northern Pacific. Hilger's ranch was near the Gates of the Mountains and he hoped to use his new launch as an excursion boat between the Gates and Great Falls. The *Townsend Tranchant* announced that the two steamers might together form a line between Townsend and Great Falls. Helena passengers could take the morning train to Townsend, board the *Rose* at 10:00 A.M., arrive at a point just past the Gates that evening and complete the journey to Great Falls the following day aboard the *Fern*. Roundtrip from Helena to Great Falls could be made in four days.

The *Rose* reached Great Falls in May of 1886 while the *Fern* still awaited her machinery, but the maiden voyage of the nimble *Rose* was not without difficulties. As Davison and Commodore Wheeler left Townsend in her wake to chart the course their own craft would later take, they caught the *Rose* "grounded on a sandbar…and spent three hours" helping her off. It was an ominous beginning.

After some financial difficulties, the *Fern* received her engines and her first voyage was scheduled for summer 1887. The crew consisted of Davison, his two sons, engineers Fred Thurston and Nat Drummond, and pilot Robert McDougall. The passenger list included Mrs. Davison, three small children and a handful of reporters. That the *Fern* was no match for the treacherous upper Missouri became quickly apparent. Two hours out of Townsend "a sandbar loomed ahead where but yesterday had run the deep river channel." The bell in the engine room sounded and McDougall fought to turn the bow, but the steamer caught a rock and there she stuck.

Passengers were temporarily put ashore and it was two days before the *Fern* again floated free. Months of charting the river had been wasted effort; the river had a "penchant for changing its course in a night." Four miles farther and she was again stranded. More than 150 miles of sand and shallows yet stood between the *Fern* and Great Falls.

The difficulties of the journey multiplied. Woodchoppers contracted to supply fuel along the way were either frightened off by Indians or their wood ricks became inaccessible because of the river's ever-changing currents. Drifting sand surrounded the boat at its mooring each night. Ferry cables were another great annoyance. Without federal authority to navigate, it was up to the crew to remove and replace troublesome cables strung across the water at every crossing.

Even so, magnificent scenery kept the passengers at the rails while elk, deer, an occasional buffalo, and even Indians watching the "fireboat" from a distance "...added a touch of danger and mystery." At the Gates of the Mountains, the *Fern* and the *Rose* steamed along in tandem for an historic moment until the more cumbersome *Fern* was left to fend for herself as the *Rose* pulled on ahead to meet her schedule.

Finally on No-

The Fern *proved why Fort Benton was the head of navigation on the Missouri.*

MONTANA HISTORICAL SOCIETY

vember 7, 1887, after weeks of dredging and towing, the *Fern* arrived at Great Falls to a hearty welcome. Paris Gibson greeted the steamer and the *Great Falls Tribune* politely called the trip "successful." In a sense it was, too, for the *Fern's* "struggle with the muddy Missouri had demonstrated for all time the fallacy of attempting to navigate the stream with vessels of her tonnage."

While the *Rose* retired in 1906 after providing countless excursionists magnificent river scenery, the *Fern* was sold and remained where she was at the end of her singular voyage. She did, however, continue to play a role in the history of the river stretch between Townsend and Great Falls. In 1892, she figured in a half-hearted argument against a proposal for a dam at Stubbs' Ferry. A Great Falls lumber company, which argued the river's navigability, was concerned about not being able to float its logs. The *Helena Herald* reported that the lumber contingent "...made some rambling statements...in regard to a certain steamer called the *Fern*....It was launched at Townsend and made the descent to Great Falls...and is there yet...." In 1946, the *Fern* once again figured in a hearing on the navigability of the upper Missouri. This time the argument was the opposite, to disprove the navigability of the Missouri River between Townsend and Great Falls in order to exempt Montana Power Company from licensing its hydroelectric dams.

Under new ownership, the *Fern* was pressed into service within more stringent boundaries, hauling small groups short distances upriver from Great Falls for picnics and other brief excursions. Her last recorded trip was in 1923, when she carried partygoers a mile and a half upstream to the Volk brewery beer garden—where Jack Dempsey was training for his fight with Tom Gibbons.

Dr. Davison admitted the failure of his venture, but he was not sorry to have undertaken it. He later moved to Utah, where he died in 1897; at his request, his body was returned to East Helena for burial. His enterprise, although not what he had envisioned, put an end to speculation and proved that the upper Missouri could "serve mankind only by harnessing it to the wheels of industry."

Copper Kings, Corruption & Satire

BY KIMBERLY MORRISON

Today, when the subjects of national political scandals are common household names, it would be easy to view Montana's own short political history in a relatively tame light, as a rather chaste and simple piece to a much larger and more complex bureaucratic puzzle. Yet one of the defining moments of Montana's past rivals even the most scandalous politics of the present—the battle for the capital of 1894, a drawn-out personal showdown that played out on a very public front.

"Capital fights" were common in the West during the late 19th century and were often noted for their highly-visible and hotly-contested campaigns. But Montana's contest between Helena and Anaconda in 1894 clearly overshadowed other such elections and, in retrospect, took on legendary proportions.

The fight actually began in 1889 at the state constitutional convention. Delegates from all parts of the new state of Montana sidestepped the issue of where to locate the state capital, instead tossing the volatile question directly into the hands of the electorate. During the 1892 election year, seven Montana cities submitted the required petition of twenty-five signatures and claimed a spot on the ballot. Those cities included Boulder, Bozeman, Butte, Deer Lodge, Great Falls, Anaconda and Helena. Voter turnout was heavy that year, and in the end, Helena led the list of challengers, earning over thirty percent of the vote; Anaconda was right at its heels, however, with a twenty-two percent margin.

Because the 1892 election failed to post a majority for any

one city, Helena and Anaconda, the top two choices, found themselves slated for a run-off vote scheduled for the 1894 general election. During the ensuing two-year period, corporate politics and personal vendettas colored the capital campaign, as the freewheeling copper kings and rivals, Marcus Daly and William Andrew Clark, injected their money, influence, and personal hostilities into the fight for the capital.

Marcus Daly, who molded and shaped his corporate fiefdom of Anaconda from its birth in 1883, had actually been involved with selecting a site for the state capital from the beginning. His ultimate goal was to immortalize Anaconda, and ultimately, his own personal success, with its selection as the state capital. William A. Clark, on the other hand, did not throw his hat into the ring for Helena until after the 1893 legislative session, when Daly's men blocked Clark's attempt to be appointed to the U.S. Senate (state legislatures selected senators until 1913). The legislative defeat was more than Clark's ego could bear, and he quickly joined forces with influential banker Samuel T. Hauser in the Helena-for-capital campaign.

The Helena versus Anaconda question dominated the Montana print media during 1894. As early as April, debates were held, and not long after, "capital committees" began sponsoring picnics, parades, and fireworks. In addition, speakers' bureaus began preaching the attributes of their chosen city. Yet legitimate campaigning took a back seat with Daly's reputation on the line against Clark's spite. It was not long before the flow of satirical propaganda and mining money began to contaminate the election.

Blistering columns appeared in state newspapers as each endorsed either Helena or Anaconda. The Clark-owned *Butte Miner* flooded its pages with editorials about Daly's tyranny in Anaconda and the Anaconda Copper Mining Company's immense power and influence. The *Miner* questioned the logic of putting the state capital into the hands of a large corporation. *Miner* editor John M. Quinn even charged that Daly had hired a number of thugs to strong-arm the public into registering and voting for Anaconda. The *Helena Weekly Herald,* meanwhile, randomly sprinkled its pages with "King Marco" and "Killing the 'Conda" satirical poems. Daly's *Anaconda Stan-*

dard vigorously fought back, charging Helena with arrogance, self-aggrandizement, and friendliness to anti-labor forces. The art of political caricatures matured during the campaign, with cartoonists depicting such symbolic characters as the "Helena Hog" and the "Anaconda Snake."

During the campaign, both sides organized strong coalitions, which tried to influence voters with money, threats, or both. During election week, five-dollar bills and free liquor were purportedly found on every street corner in Butte, Anaconda and Helena if potential voters would lend their ears and their votes. In addition, both sides charged each other with importing voters for their respective sides. According to historian Dave Walter, the electorate, in turn, took advantage of this corruption, with some men forming "capital groups" and selling their votes in blocks to the highest bidder. By the time that election day arrived, Clark and Daly spent an estimated $50.00 per vote.

When November 6, 1894, finally rolled around, voters went to the polls in scores, compiling a turnout of over 90 percent. Although for two days the actual vote tabulations were too close to call, the *Helena Herald* proclaimed victory on November 7, stating that "Helena will get the capital as sure as the sun rises in the east and sets in the west." The *Butte Miner* did the same, proclaiming "THREE CHEERS! THE PEOPLE ARE SUPREME! THE CITIZENSHIP OF MONTANA IS VINDICATED! TYRANNY HAS REACHED ITS WATERLOO." Helena was declared the victor the following day.

And what of the Copper Kings? Well, William Clark celebrated into the wee hours of the morning on November 12, the day set aside for the victory celebration in Helena. And Marcus Daly, after conceding defeat to Helena, quickly lost interest in the town of Anaconda, limping instead to his mansion in the Bitterroot for the remainder of the 19th century. For Clark, the campaign of 1894 ended with a thrilling victory; for Daly a devastating defeat.

Montana's Contingent of Coxey's Army

by Leanne Kurtz

The 1890s were an economically desperate time. So desperate, in fact, that hundreds of thousands of thinking, yet jobless, men placed their faith in a guy who had named his son "Legal Tender." In 1892, Jacob Sechler Coxey, an active populist and quarry operator from Massillon, Ohio, began to mobilize struggling laborers across the country. As the silver industry tarnished during the Panic of 1893, so did the driving force behind Butte's economy, with hundreds of silver workers out of work. These men, suddenly with a lot of time on their hands, looked to Jacob Coxey and his "General" in Montana, William Hogan, to help them regain some semblance of financial stability. They did not know that they would soon be led on a great adventure across Montana, pursued by a federal marshal, arrested, and tried, eventually becoming temporary residents of a soggy, muddy Helena fairgrounds.

Jacob Coxey recognized the severity of America's economic difficulties, and, in 1892, proposed the "Good Roads Bill," asking Congress for a $500 million appropriation to employ laborers to expand and improve the country's road system, while infusing the ailing economy with a much-needed shot of funds. Congress rejected Coxey's proposal while the financial situation continued to worsen. His next effort came in the spring of 1894 with the resurrection of the roads bill and the drafting of the "Noninterest-bearing Bonds Bill," a measure he felt would achieve the same objectives yet address problems found in the "Good Roads Bill." To illustrate the need for both pieces of legislation, Coxey called on 100,000 of America's unemployed to mobilize and march on Washington. Coxey's own Ohio legion was the only group to complete the trip. Both the roads bill and the bonds bill failed, Coxey and his minions were arrested at the capitol for walking on the grass, and the troops eventually scattered to the four winds.

In its planning stages, word of the great gathering at the nation's capital did not go unheard in Montana, where copper and silver miners alike had seen their livelihoods dissolve with the collapse of the metals industry. As Coxey's Ohio contingent wended its way to Washington, General William Hogan organized his Montana troops in Butte and tried through several avenues to win local government and corporate sponsorship for a trip to Washington. His attempts failed and Hogan's army found itself stuck in a camp near the Northern Pacific railyards outside Butte.

In the early morning hours of April 24, 1894, a small group of Hogan's men broke into the railway roundhouse, fired up a Northern Pacific engine, attached a few coal cars and box cars, loaded up the rest of the hearty voyagers and headed east. Federal Marshal William McDermott, in true Tommy-Lee-Jones-in-*The-Fugitive* style, directed the pursuit of the wayward train, which was barreling toward Washington at excessive rates of speed. Cheering crowds and new recruits greeted the speeding train all along its route across the southern half of Montana. When the 350-man–strong army reached Billings, McDermott and his seventy-five deputies made their move. A fight ensued, resulting in injury to several deputies and the death of a Billings citizen. The Coxeyites overcame the remaining federal officials, took their weapons and continued on their journey.

This called for serious measures: the big guns—the United States Army. Three companies of troops stationed at Forts Custer and Keogh met and surrounded the train upon its arrival at Forsyth. The Coxeyites surrendered without further incident and Marshal McDermott sent over 300 of them to the federal courts in Helena, where the Northern Pacific charged the leaders with larceny. The rest of the dispirited troops appeared before the judge, thirty at a time. The judge released each group after they promised to never again steal a Northern Pacific train.

He also informed them that the Northern Pacific, understandably miffed, would not allow any of them passage out of the state on its rail network. A May 1894 account of the courtroom scene states, "When Judge Knowles pronounced the words that made them free men once more an audible sigh arose from more than one throat as if a mighty burden had been lifted from their

Camped at Forsyth, Montana's Coxeyites predict success.

shoulders...Some few remained in front of the Gold block, not knowing what to do or where to go, apparently helpless now that liberty to do as they pleased had been granted." Now, the fallen warriors were Helena's problem.

The newly-freed Coxeyites set up camp at the fairgrounds and held marches and meetings in downtown Helena. They hadn't given up their dream of making it to Washington in time for the gathering of their compatriots and asked Helenans for their help. Helena had more than enough on its plate, as the town was in the midst of the bitter battle with Anaconda for state capital designation, but town leaders did not want to appear uncharitable. The refugees at the fairgrounds received food from local philanthropists, but everyone involved knew it couldn't last and that help from the railroads was out of the question. Soon, an unnamed Helenan had an idea. If the townspeople provided food and materials, they could send the army to Fort Benton, where they would construct their own barges and float out of the state and out of the state's proverbial hair.

Helena's Mayor Weed made it clear that the town had no intention of "dumping" its problem on Fort Benton, but his attempts fell a bit short. "The Coxeys are coming," reads a May 30 Fort Benton *River Press* column, "Rumors to that effect have been published in previous issues, but now it seems an assured fact that the Montana disciples of General Coxey will congregate at Fort Benton and build boats here, and then float gaily down the old, historic Missouri, from the head of navigation to the mouth...Just think of it! Boats and grub furnished, and free water passage for over 2,500 miles with nothing to do but float, eat, sleep, admire the scenery and discuss the Wilson bill. Who wouldn't be a Coxeyite?"

Wayward Coxeyites from all over Montana arrived in Fort Benton during the week of May 29 to build boats. By early June, the men had constructed ten large flat vessels and drifted down the mighty Missouri and out of Montana. Towns along the way fed them and ushered them out of the city limits as quickly as possible. Their once-enthusiastic crusade ended in a whimper as the troops eventually dispersed during the Missouri voyage.

Coxey's Army, a grassroots movement that influenced thousands of despondent unemployed men to take such extreme measures as stealing a train to improve their situation, quickly faded from the national political scene. Coxey himself took to growing fruit in the state of Washington and his followers roamed the countryside, seeking whatever work was available. Though they didn't persuade Congress to see things their way, in the process of trying, the Montana contingent of Coxey's Army had an adventure they would never forget.

MARK TWAIN APPEARS IN HELENA

BY DAVE WALTER

Few of us have escaped the fantasy of "the time machine." In particular, history buffs are prone to this flight of fantasy. What if we really could control a time-warp device to transport us into another time slot—either past or future—simply by dialing the month, day, and year on the calibrator? What if we really could choose a time and drop ourselves right in the middle of that lifestyle?

If Helenans possessed such a "time machine," their calculations would be simple for August 3, 1995. Merely by setting the dial for a century ago, they would transport themselves into a Helena community perched on the brink of a rare opportunity.

For, at 8:00 P.M. on August 3, 1895, Samuel Langhorne Clemens (better known to his readers as "Mark Twain") would take the stage at Ming's Opera House on North Jackson Street. And Helenans in droves would snub the renowned performer by ignoring his appearance!

Helena, in 1895, continued to reel from the national Crash of 1893. Montana silver mining had all but ceased. Two Helena banks and scores of businesses recently had closed their doors; two other banks teetered on the edge of failure. Still, the town maintained a population of almost 11,500. Only one year earlier it had defeated Anaconda in the raucous "Capital Fight" to determine the permanent capital of Montana.

The "Queen City of the Rockies" continued to serve as the financial, political, and cultural center of the young state.

Ming's Opera House—today's Consistory Shrine Temple on North Jackson—hosted Twain in 1895.

Wealthy survivors of the Crash of 1893 busily built mansions on the upper west side and in the Lenox Addition. The town boasted seven newspapers, a well-developed trolley system, and eighteen daily trains. Helena became a necessary stop for the national artist touring the state, whether that be Sarah Bernhardt, or Alexander Salvini, or Helena Modjeska.

Ming's Opera House—the remodeled building now known as the Consistory Shrine Temple—had opened in 1880 and immediately became Helena's primary showplace. In 1895 theater manager James L. Ming hosted touring "name" actors and actresses, repertory drama companies, musical-variety shows, operatic productions, renowned vocalists, and circuit-riding lecturers. The Torbett Concert Company immediately preceded Twain's one-night stand on August 3, and touring comedian J.K. "Fritz" Emmett, starring in his own production of "Fritz in a Madhouse," followed two nights later.

Samuel Clemens arrived in Helena rather early in a fifteen-month world tour that would take him across the U.S. to San Francisco and then to the Fiji Islands, Australia, India, South Africa, and England. The sixty-year-old Clemens had agreed to this extended tour as a way of repaying massive debts incurred from failed investments in a publishing company and in a mechanical typesetter. His excursion proved financially successful and, in 1897, he released a volume of reminiscences based on the tour, entitled *Following the Equator.*

Clemens travelled the American leg of this tour with his wife Livy and his twenty-one-year-old daughter Clara. Noted theatrical manager Major J.B. Pond and his wife Martha completed the party. The major earned a 25 percent commission on all fees in return for handling the various aspects of the tour.

In Montana, Pond had scheduled Clemens to appear in Great Falls, Butte, Anaconda, Helena, and Missoula between July 31 and August 6. The author's health remained a concern to Pond, since Clemens had not recovered fully from a painful carbuncle on his leg that had forced him to bed for six weeks during the preceding spring.

At each of the Montana stops, Clemens presented a rambling program of humorous stories, woven together with social commentary. Although billed as "a lecture," the two-hour performance carried a much more informal, anecdotal tone. The basic format included:

(1) "My First Theft"
(2) "The Celebrated Jumping Frog"
(3) "The Character of the Blue Jay"
(4) "A Fancy Dress Incident"
(5) "Bit Off More Than He Could Chew"
(6) "Tom Sawyer's Crusade"

The Clemens entourage registered at the Hotel Helena on Saturday morning, August 3. Located on Grand Street, just above Main, the Helena advertised itself as "the Only First-Class Hotel in the City." The *Helena Daily Herald* had posted a newsman in the lobby, who reported (August 3, 1895):

> To the casual observer, as he stood in the corridor facing the parlor, hat in hand, running his fingers through his long, curly locks, now almost gray, he was any-

thing but a humorist. On the contrary, he appeared to be a gentleman of great gravity, a statesman or a man of vast business interests.

The dark blue eyes are as clear as crystal and the keenest of glances shoots from them whenever he speaks....The kindly smile that lights up his face and the general appearance of happy abandon proclaim an author who is no bookworm. He talks easily and quietly, yet with marked deliberation.

Prior to reaching Helena, the well-known western writer had filled theaters in Great Falls, Butte, and Anaconda. The *Great Falls Tribune* (August 1, 1895) cooed that "the best audience that ever attended an entertainment of a similar nature in Great Falls listened to Mark Twain's ninety-minute talk at the Opera House last night and thoroughly enjoyed the entertainment." The *Butte Daily Miner* reported (August 1, 1895):

Mark Twain appeared at Maguire's Opera House tonight to the largest and most fashionable audience since [Sarah] Bernhardt was here. The entertainment was a great success. Peals of laughter and sounds of applause greeted the eminent speaker every few minutes.

At Ming's Opera House on Saturday night, however, Clemens (fashionably bedecked in his familiar pure-white suit) played to only a partial house. Major Pond—aware of Helena's reputation for cultural pretensions and only "high-brow entertainment"—remarked (*Eccentricities of Genius*, 1900):

In Helena the people did not care for lectures. They all liked "Mark" and enjoyed meeting him, but there was no public enthusiasm [i.e., ticket sales] for the man who had made the early history of that mining country romantic and famous all the world over.

After the performance, Helena dignitaries escorted Clemens to the Montana Club, where they held a closed reception. Major Pond noted:

At the Montana Club, "Mark" met many old friends and acquaintances, who entertained him grandly. Some of them had come all the way from Virginia City, Nevada, on purpose to see him, an old comrade from the 1860s grown famous.

"Mark" simply bests the world in telling stories—although we found some very bright lights here. There were present former U.S. Senator Wilbur Fisk Sanders, politician Major Martin Maginnis, publisher Hugh McQuaid, merchant A.J. Seligman, U.S. District Judge Hiram P. Knowles, hotelmen D.A. Walker and Dr. C.K. Cole, financier A.J. Steele, and mining engineer Frank L. Sizer....."Mark" walked from the Club to the Hotel, up quite a mountain, the first hard walk he has had. He stands the light air well, and he is getting strong."

On the next day, a blistering-hot Sunday, the party remained in Helena to rest before taking the Northern Pacific express to Missoula. The Major explained:

The dry, burning sun makes life almost intolerable, so that there has been hardly a soul on the streets all day...."Mark" lay around on the floor of his room all day, reading and writing in his notebook and smoking.

In the gloaming, Dr. Cole, with his trotters, drove "Mark" and Mrs. Clemens out to the Broadwater, about four miles. The heat gave way to a delicious balmy breeze that reinvigorated everybody. How delightful are these summer evenings in the Rocky Mountains!

On Monday morning, August 5, the Clemens party left Helena from the Northern Pacific depot. That evening the humorist performed for a packed house at the Bennett Theater in Missoula—a crowd described *(Daily Missoulian,* August 6) as "large, select, fashionable, and thoroughly in touch with their intellectual entertainer." From Missoula, Clemens' tour led west, into Washington.

But Samuel Clemens had mounted the stage at Ming's Opera House to find almost one half of the seats empty. When we master the use of "the time machine," perhaps it will permit scores of present-day Helenans to see "Mark Twain" perform at the Ming and to give the dignitary that standing-room-only crowd he deserved. Perhaps that "time machine" will help us redeem the town's reputation—after snubbing one of the country's most accomplished humorists.

UP IN SMOKE

❧

BY ELLEN BAUMLER

On the night of April 28, 1903, Helena witnessed the most spectacular fire the town had seen since the long-ago 1870s. On that snowy April night, flames rapidly consumed the famed Montana Club. As it became clear in the following weeks that the fire had been intentionally set, a bizarre drama unfolded on the pages of the *Daily Independent.*

The original 1890s Montana Club building was designed by Helena architect J.M. Paulsen and had long been touted as Montana's finest showpiece. The handsome seven-story edifice, known from coast to coast, had served to advertise Helena as a "prosperous and progressive" city. The event was therefore of more than local interest. The fire was discovered at about 11:00 P.M. on the building's seventh floor. Winds that whipped through the gulch that night helped fuel the inferno to such intensity that within fifteen minutes it was clearly out of control. While firefighters tried unsuccessfully to reach the flames with their equipment, the fire simply ate the building floor by floor. By three o'clock in the morning, there was nothing left to burn. The fire had been so fierce that, although the water pressure was good at the time, it was not enough. Burst hoses, dense smoke, an insufficient number of water lines and the building's height all contributed to the hopelessness of the situation.

The following day, as snow fell on the still-smoldering ruins, the loss was reported at $150,000 to the building and its furnishings. It had been insured for $65,000. Two commercial offices on the ground floor, occupied by the Helena Water Works and an insurance agency, were also a total loss. Ironically, these businesses represented the two things the club lacked in sufficient quantity: water to fight the fire and insurance to pay for the awful damage.

The original Montana Club building sometime between 11 p.m. April 28, 1903, and 3:00 the following morning.

At first it seemed "scarcely credible" that the fire had been intentionally set. However, another fire a few nights previous led club members to be suspicious. That fire had started in the base-ment and was quickly extinguished. Club members hired a sea-soned detective to conduct a quiet investigation. After carefully going over the long list of guests and employees, he finally fo-cused on the fourteen-year-old son of ten-year club employee Julian Anderson. Young Harry Anderson had been on the job as elevator boy for just a few days when the first fire occurred. Members found him hiding in the basement where that fire orig-inated. Toy, the club's cook who had discovered the second blaze, reported that he had heard someone moving about on the seventh floor near the elevator. While the investigation of this circumstantial evidence was ongoing, Harry remained in the club's employ and had no idea he was under suspicion.

Meanwhile, two other unexplained fires occurred in Helena the following month. Both of these fires damaged buildings owned by Edward G. Cole, proprietor of a secondhand store on Broadway. One of these buildings was a stable on Hoback and the other was variously reported to be either the house or barn at 27 Spencer Street. William Smith, a night watchman at Cole's store and a resident at the Spencer Street property, reported to the police that Harry Anderson had claimed responsibility for starting the Spencer Street fire. During the ensuing investigation of the Cole fires, Police Chief Thomas Travis turned up some other damaging evidence. It seems that Harry had warned Mrs. Cole of a possible fire. He himself had turned in the stable fire alarm. He had been waiting at the Seventh Ward fire station at 803 Breckenridge when the Spencer Street alarm had come in and rode to the blaze in the fire wagon. Further, on the morning before the Montana Club fire, Anderson was at the same fire station and commented that there would likely be another fire at the club house. He claimed that he had smelled smoke in the elevator and believed that the first fire was still smoldering in the basement.

As the investigation progressed, it became evident that young Anderson had a peculiar predilection for being at the scene of fires. He liked to hang around the firemen and their equipment. He was a familiar sight at alarms and the firemen often allowed him to ride with them in the wagon and exercise the horses while the men worked. In addition, when the African Methodist Episcopal Church at Hoback and Fifth Avenue burned a few months before, Anderson had reportedly been seen in the basement not fifteen minutes before the fire was discovered. The origin of that fire, however, seems never to have been fully investigated.

At this point, Chief Travis and the detective working on the club fire compared notes. The pieces of this strange story began to fall into place. Anderson was arrested without incident, still on the job at the Sam Word house, which once stood at 626 Madison Avenue, where the Montana Club had set up temporary quarters. Chief Travis escorted him to the station without incident, as the *Daily Independent* reported, "Clad in knickerbockers, neatly dressed and looking scarce his 14 years." The one-time Central School student seemed to possess "all the coolness of the experienced," but according to those who knew him, he had always been a "quiet, peaceable lad." With the promise of a sentence to reform school and no other punishment, Anderson confessed to having started all four fires. He apparently had an "uncontrollable desire to see the horses run and to help the firemen work." In the discussion of both the Montana Club fires and the stable fire, the youth told Chief Travis that the sight of an old gunny sack and small pieces of wood tinder led to an irresistible temptation to strike a match and ignite them. At the Spencer Street fire, Anderson admitted that he had seen two men in the house, "…and I thought it would be a good thing to scare them." He went on, "I saw some hay sticking out of a barn and I took a match and lit it.…I did not…mean to do any damage, all that I intended to do was to have the horses run. I thought that they [the firemen] would be at the place before any damage was done."

On the morning of June 9, Judge Henry C. Smith sentenced the fourteen-year-old to the state reform school at Miles City. He was to remain there until the age of twenty-one. Judge Smith admonished the young defendant to behave or face further charges in the Cole matter and be sent to the penitentiary. He elaborated, "I would not like to send you to the penitentiary because if I did, you would come in contact with all kinds of hardened criminals.…I want you to try to be a good boy…and get these ideas of burning things out of your head because if you don't, you will certainly come to a bad end." Anderson left with the sheriff that afternoon on the eastbound train to Miles City. It is uncertain whether he ever returned to Helena. Directories, census rolls and cemetery records of the following decades provide no further information about his fate.

Part of the epilogue of the Montana Club fire is, as Helenans already know, that the membership rebuilt its quarters. Only the stone at street level predates the 1903 conflagration. The other half of the story's end is that Harry's father, Julian Anderson, became one of Helena's most beloved characters, employed continuously by the Montana Club as bartender *par excellence* until his retirement in 1953. While local stories about Julian Anderson's sixty-year tenure figure prominently in the colorful history of the Montana Club, the unfortunate acts of his son have been quietly forgotten.

HELENA IN THE MOVIES

BY LEANNE KURTZ

Celebrity mongers among us were disappointed in 1996 to learn that Oliver Stone had decided against bringing Norman Maclean's *Young Men and Fire* to the big screen. Even after a visit to Hap's, Helena's famous railroad bar, reportedly to look at the vintage ceiling, Stone decided the story was not well suited to the motion picture medium.

Through the years, Montana has played host to numerous Hollywood productions and they keep coming. Helena itself was even featured (with a substitute town appearing on screen) in *Legends of the Fall,* and our burg was mentioned in Robert Redford's adaptation of Maclean's *A River Runs Through It.* With all this exposure, however, Helena has had to settle for news crews craning for a shot at the elusive Unabomber suspect rather than Hollywood film crews picking actors out of the crowd and spreading their wealth among local businesses.

In the spring of 1920, to everyone's delight, a little Hollywood visited Helena, and did just that. At the behest of *The Helena Independent,* Los Angeles' Hudris Film Company traveled to the Capital City, cast all local talent, and shot a movie entitled *A Romance of Helena.* The photoplay ran for three days at the Marlow Theater alongside two major Hollywood productions, *Red Hot Dollars* starring Charles Ray and *The Gingham Girl.*

News of the production first appeared in *The Independent* on March 25, 1920. All Helenans were encouraged to submit applications and audition before the film's director. *The Independent* promised prospective actors and actresses that no favoritism would be shown, and no experience was necessary, as "the director is a stranger to the people of Helena," and he will "pick [cast members] only by merit as he sees fit." The announcement stated that thousands of young aspiring actors and actresses write to film companies each year in hopes of breaking into the business. With this movie under their belts, the article suggested, Helena novices would have something to show movie executives to prove they, in fact, could act. After its screening at the Marlow, the article read, "the film will be loaned to those who take part; and they will be permitted to send the picture to regular releasing companies at Los Angeles." While entertainment sections in the papers recounted the sordid details of Mary Pickford's troubled marriage to Douglas Fairbanks, Sr., Helenans were gearing up to become silver screen sensations in their own right.

The Independent assured its readers that no expense would be spared during filming and promised a polished, professional product, for at the head of Hudris Film Company was "William Harris, Jr.,...brother of the late Henry B. Harris, the New York theatrical manager, who was lost on the *Titanic*...[and] the public is assured that this production will have attending it all the dignity of a high class production." Apparently, sinking with the *Titanic* lent credibility in the theater business. On April 1, 1920, the cameras started rolling with Helena's own A.I. "Daddy" Reeves as "Papa Atherton," and Marlow Theater cashier, Miss Lavina Holshue, as the heroine.

The Independent provides no thorough description of the movie's plot, but one can glean from the settings and the accounts of filming published in the paper, that all the familiar themes were visited: boy meets girl, good versus evil, and a climactic fight scene. The April 3 edition of the paper reports, "BATTLE BETWEEN HERO AND VILLAIN CONCLUDES, PORTRAYAL OF 'ROMANCE IN HELENA' SCENE OF A NEWSPAPER EXTRA IS TOO DING BUSTED LIVELY, PEOPLE THINK IT'S THE REAL THING." A wedding in front of the Cathedral and a street fight near Sands Brothers' store attracted plenty of attention from Helena residents unused to such events occurring in their quiet town.

"One of the scenes," read the paper, "where a lot of newsboys ran out of the office of *The Independent* with arm loads of papers, came nearly being an April 2 joke. People on the street thought an extra had been issued and the boys had to fight to keep people from buying the old papers they were using in the scene." A cold, wintry spring made appearing in shirt sleeves and summer costumes a special challenge for the new thespians. An editorial in *The Independent* quotes a "village pessimist, whose disposition has been warped as badly as a lettuce leaf fried in hot lard" as complaining, "That there film...ought to be showed sometime in August when the sweat is stickin' your B.V.D.'s to yer hide. It might redoos th' temperature." The editorial agrees, "It is discouraging to stand around with your nose the color of a beet and leaky at that, humped up in an overcoat and a fur cap, both of which you must lay aside when you appear in a June wedding." During one of the particularly chilly days of filming, said "pessimist" reportedly asked the director to change the movie's name from *A Romance in Helena* to *Snowballin' in Hell e na.* The editorial concludes

"Blowing a trumpet blast on his nasal bugle, the director said it was 'jake' with him and then he shifted his megaphone in the direction of the luckless young man in summer attire, frescoed with icicles, and told him to 'put some pep' in his lovemaking. 'Darn the Prohibitionists,' chattered the young man, apropos of nothing in particular. 'Amen!' chorused the cast, the mob, the director and the camera man and the spectators."

The trauma appeared to have been worth it. From April 20 to April 23, *A Romance of Helena* packed the Marlow and captivated the crowds. LOCAL THESPIANS SCORE, read *The Independent* in a rave review of the film. The comedy scenes sent audiences into "paroxysms of merriment."

The proposal scene," gushed the review, "well, a wrestling match is a mild affair compared with the caresses lavished by Ed Doll on pretty Lavina Holshue."

"As a kisser, Ed scores heavily," another review remarked, we hope only after speaking first with the pretty Miss Lavina Holshue. The opening night article concluded, "The picture ends with a wild kaleidoscopic effect of Sixth and Main on a busy day in which the Helena police rival the Keystone cops for speedy work...Never did a big audience pour out of a theater at the conclusion of a picture or a show in a more hilarious humor."

It is likely that *A Romance of Helena* did not enthrall audiences nationwide, nor would it probably have been an Oscar contender, had there been such accolades in 1920. The production brought a small piece of Hollywood to Helena, though, and dazzled local audiences with its professional quality. Attempts to locate copies of the film were unsuccessful, and it is possible that the celluloid has long since gone the way of the Marlow Theater, given the lack of preservation techniques.

But it would indeed be fun to see Helena's own Ed Doll scoring heavily.

GOLD IN THE GULCH

WHERE WAS THE
FIRST GOLD FOUND?

❧

BY VIVIAN A. PALADIN

Late in August 1993, a man named T.J. Carnes came to
Helena from his home in Albertville, Alabama, and he had a
mission. It was to find a plaque that he had been told marked
the spot where, on July 14, 1864, a gold strike rich enough to
launch Montana's capital city was made. Carnes' story and his
picture appeared on the front page of the *Independent Record*'s
issue of Thursday, August 26, 1993. It was an appealing story
because it had some romantic and historical overtones, and it
had the ring of truth. But it also struck a note which was jarring at the time and remains so today.

The visitor from Alabama came to Helena in 1993 because
he is from the same small town as was one of the four "Discoverers," mistakenly called to this day the Four Georgians. The
Alabaman was D.J. Miller, a dedicated and persistent miner
who had spent quite a lot of time in California before coming
to Montana Territory. His goal was to find enough gold so he
could return to Albertville and claim as his bride Miss Mary
Henry, whose wealthy father would not approve the marriage
until Miller was able to "support his daughter in the fashion
she is accustomed to."

The story of Miller's romance and its happy ending made
for pleasant reading, and a number of archival sources indi-
cate that the story is true. The jarring note came in a sidebar
to the story entitled "Founders' plaque a secret?" Carnes told
reporter Grant Sasek of the *IR* that he could find no one who
could tell him where the plaque was that marked the spot where
his fellow townsman's dreams came true. "The person I talked
to at the Chamber of Commerce never heard of the plaque,"

Carnes said. "The Historical Society had heard of it but didn't know where it was."

Failing to get any guidance from those he asked, Carnes made a pilgrimage to Last Chance Gulch and adjoining streets and walked about by himself until he found it. Apparently then telling his story to the *IR*, he pleaded with reporter Sasek to "do me a favor and let folks know where it is." The visitor was photographed beside the plaque which he found bolted to the side of the Helena Abstract and Title Co. building at the corner of Sixth and Fuller Avenues—the Montana Club building.

In making his inquiries, Carnes may well have been talking to younger, perhaps temporary summer personnel. For in truth, many who have been concerned about Helena's history have known it was there, and has been for some seventy years. But anyone, newcomer or long-time resident, can be excused for a lack of knowledge about this modest bronze marker, for it is a dubious monument at best. Research, archival investigation and even geological observations all suggest that this is not the place where pieces of gold heavy enough to "make the pan ring" were first found on the evening of July 14, 1864.

The spoken and written testimony of one of the discoverers, Reginald (Bob) Stanley, reinforces, perhaps more than any other source, the conclusion that this thrilling event took place a short distance west (or in back) of the long narrow Colwell Building, built in 1887 to fit the mining claim terrain. Located at 62 South Main near the southern end of today's walking mall, it is one of the important historic buildings saved and restored after the demolitions and drastic changes of the Urban Renewal programs of the 1970s.

An unusually erudite man, Reginald Stanley returned to his home in England a few years after the discoveries in Last Chance Gulch. He was the first recorder of mining claims, a fact engraved on his tombstone in Nuneaton, England, where he died in 1914 at the age of seventy-six. He stayed in Last Chance Gulch long enough to see the camp named Helena and to mine his gold and see it safely to Philadelphia for minting. He returned to England to invest and prosper in his family's brick and tile business.

Stanley returned to Helena in 1883, gratified but not surprised at the growth of the gold camp that by now was territorial capital of Montana and in another few years would be its state capital. "I had a presentiment that something of the sort might be in the future," he later wrote. "I remember climbing the foothills, to enjoy the brilliant sunset and glorious view across the Prickly Pear Valley."

Besides his visit, Stanley corresponded with Helena people through the years, especially the Sanders family. In 1909, he was invited back to Helena to help the city welcome President Taft and attend a meeting of the Montana Pioneers. Expressing his regrets, Stanley once more described the evening of July 14 when,

> *after a feed, my partners dug some holes near the mouth of the gulch, [while] I took pick, shovel and pan and made my way upstream looking for a promising bar, on which to put down a hole likely to have bedrock...There was little to distinguish the gulch from many others we had seen, a stream rippled under gravel banks, bordered with chokecherry and sarvus-berry bushes, the low hills on either side rising steeper as the gulch entered the mountain range. I commenced a hole on a bar (the opposite side of the gulch from where the first National Bank was afterwards erected) and put it down to the bedrock—some six or seven feet deep—taking a pan of gravel from the bottom. I clambered out, and panned it in the little stream close by. Nuggets!! that made the pan ring, and a very refreshing sound it was. We set to, and dug holes everywhere after that, took our time, and did extremely well. We chose what we thought the best ground. Then, being out of flour, Cowan and Crab went to Alder Gulch to get a supply and bring back a whipsaw to cut our sluice boxes...*

A blacktop parking lot now covers the discovery site as well as the short, narrow Wall Street where Sam Hauser established his first First National Bank in 1866. The stone building he erected at the site in 1869 also housed the Assay Office and

The Colwell Building was built in 1888 to the narrow measure of a mining claim. Among many businesses it housed was Weggenman's Market from 1946 to 1972. The parking lot at left of this picture is the site of the Last Chance Gulch strike.

the headquarters of King and Gillette, who operated a toll road north of Helena that passed through the same spectacular canyon as does today's Interstate.

Since there is compelling evidence to believe that this where the "colours, colours, colours" described by Stanley turned to gold heavy enough to ring a miner's pan, it is difficult to understand why a panel of distinguished citizens decided that it took place at the corner of Fuller and Sixth, at least a tenth of a mile to the north.

It is well first of all to quote the words engraved on the plaque:

Discovery of Gold in Last Chance Gulch
On this placer mining claim gold was discovered on July 14, 1864, by John Cowan and John Crab of Georgia, Bob Stanley of London, England, and D.J. Miller

of California, known as "The Georgians," who were returning from an unsuccessful prospecting expedition to the Kootenai country. This district was called Last Chance Gulch until October 30, 1864, when it was named Helena. This memorial to the achievements of these pioneers is erected by the Historical Society of Montana and the Society of Montana Pioneers. SI MONUMENTUM REQUIRIS CIRCUMSPICE.

(English translation: "If you would see the monuments of these men, look about you.")

It should be pointed out that the plaque says "on this mining claim." The four discoverers took pains to claim for themselves the best prospects, with Reginald Stanley busily recording them. Thus it is highly likely that, after the initial strike closer to the mouth of the gulch to the south, the richest ground proved to be downstream to the north, ground now in the heart of downtown Helena. The following essay describes the work of a commission named in 1920 by the Historical Society and the Montana Pioneers to determine where the gold discovery was made. Their findings, completed in 1921, resulted in the bronze plaque that many residents and visitors are unaware exists. No longer included in walking or motorized tours of the city, the plaque inspires few people to walk around and find it as did T.J. Carnes of Albertville, Alabama, in 1993.

COMMISSION NAMES OTHER GOLD SITE

BY VIVIAN A. PALADIN

The precise place along Last Chance Gulch where the first nuggets struck the gold pans of four discouraged miners on July 14, 1864, was not nearly as important to them as it later became to others. The primary concerns of John S. Cowan of Georgia, John Crab of Iowa, D.J. Miller of Alabama and Reginald (Bob) Stanley of Nuneaton, England, were to claim the best ground, record their claims, defend them against the greedy encroachment of others, and above all, work the ground they had claimed along tiny Last Chance Creek.

"Men would come and men would go," Reginald Stanley wrote forty-five years later from his home in England, "but we kept on digging and sluicing out the gold. Occasionally roving bands of Indians would pay us a visit. Besides stealing our horses they did not interfere with us. They would perch themselves on the high bank of the gulch and watch us, for hours at a time, toiling in the hot sun, no doubt thinking what fools we were…"

In later years, when the first attempts were made to place the site of discovery, the gulch had drastically changed. By now, Main Street was slightly east of the original path of the gulch. Trees had been cut away, hills that ranged both east and west were sluiced down, streets were excavated in some cases and filled in as much as thirty feet above the original bed in many others. "Ask a dozen real old-timers and you may be told of as many as a half dozen different places as the site of the discovery, and one may be a half a mile from another," wrote Watson Boyle in a feature article published in the *Hele-*

na *Independent* on Sunday, August 26, 1917. This was fifty-three years after the find, and none of the four discoverers was alive. But there were a number of "most intelligent men" still living in Helena who had launched businesses as early as 1865. They, according to Boyle, "frankly admit their ignorance of its precise location." The public record was of little use. There had been no newspapers printed here at the time, and the earliest record books of mine locations and other documents that had been kept were destroyed in fires, the most notable of which occurred in 1869, 1872 and 1874. Boyle's 1917 article pointed out that a few years earlier, one George L. Ramsey "undertook to locate definitely the site of the discovery and obtained the assistance of a number of well known pioneers to help in his effort." Ramsey's conclusions were printed in a pamphlet sponsored by the Union Bank and Trust Company, and they were the same as those reached by a special commission appointed in 1920 by the Historical Society of Montana and the Society of Montana Pioneers: "The first pay diggings were sluiced on a spot of ground now covered by the northeast corner of the Montana club building." Ramsey admitted that many disputed his findings, and the 1917 article pointed out that theories about the location ranged from the site of the present City-County Building at the head of Sixth, to near the corner of Sixth and Main where the Gold Block once was, to Park Street near Edwards (a close guess), Jackson near Broadway, and finally to "the hillside east of Main street north, between the Mitchell and Steamboat blocks."

Boyle deplored this range of supposition, pointing out that "no such uncertainty exists as to the place of the discovery of gold in Alder Gulch (Virginia City) which is marked by a monument that was recently erected." Before all the old timers go, he said, "it is fitting that the prevailing doubt as to the place where the discovery was made…should be cleaned up so that if it shall be marked the right place will be selected."

The full page feature then went on to tell the story of the discovery. Recounting again the story of how the four prospectors had found numerous colors, but only colors, in this area before deciding to try their luck farther north as far as the Marias, Boyle wrote, "Up the Dearborn they went, and on to the headwaters of the Teton and Marias rivers, where they found excellent prospects of grizzly bears, but none of gold. Concluding they were out of the gold country, they turned south and took their course for Alder Gulch."

But they remembered the gulch on the Prickly Pear where they had seen such promising colors. They began calling it their "last chance," for they were by now dangerously low on provisions and even lower on hope.

George Ramsey's 1921 commission decided the Last Chance strike was made under the northeast corner of today's Montana Club building.

They reached the spot again one afternoon, on or about the 15th of July [it was actually the 14th] and made their camp a short distance up the gulch near to where the First National Bank was built in 1866. [The site of today's Colwell Building.] That evening they put two good holes down to the bedrock, one on each side of the creek. When the rock was reached the hole on the north side was found to prospect well…Several flat pieces of gold that would weigh quite half a dollar were taken out; there was no mistake about it—the little nuggets fell into the ringing pan with a music particularly theirs, a sound grateful to the ears of our four wanderers. The gravel prospected to the top of the ground and they were experienced enough to know that at last Dame Fortune had kindly smiled upon them. Long into the night they sat around the fire, too pleased to turn in. Within each bosom had bloomed the hope of making the homestake and seeing friends and kindred once again; and when they slept it was to dream of civilization and a good square meal.

Boyle then made an observation that should have served to guide the efforts of those who later claimed, with the participation and blessings of some of Helena's most prominent citizens, that the site was quite a distance to the north, at the site of the imposing Montana Club building, on the corner of Sixth and Fuller. Here is what Boyle wrote:

It will be noticed that in relating the finding of colors in Last Chance Gulch before the party went north, colors not rich enough to cause them to locate a claim, Stanley writes, "No discovery had yet been made in Last Chance Gulch."...The confusion of thought or recollection about the place where the discovery was made may be due, in part, to mistaking the place where colors were found, for the place where the discovery of pay dirt was made by the party on their return from the north. They did not seek gold where they had previously found colors, but made their camp a short distance up the gulch, near where the First National Bank was built in 1866.

In 1926, the *Record-Herald* published a full page feature headlined "Pioneers Mark 62nd Anniversary of Gold Discovery." A gala banquet was held at the Placer Hotel with hosts Norman B. Holter, Dr. O.M. Landstrum, Charles B. Power and David R. Wallace honoring the "stalwart empire builders who are fast passing into history," but who "represent the type of sterling character on which Montana has builded."

An adjoining article tells the story of the bronze tablet attached to the wall of the Montana Club in time to mark the 60th anniversary of the gold discovery in 1924. A commission consisting of George L. Ramsey, Mrs. C.B. Nolan, John H.

Shober, Senator T.C. Power, and Maurice S. Weiss was appointed in 1920 by C.B. Power on behalf of the Historical Society of Montana and W.A. Clark on behalf of the Society of Montana Pioneers.

The commission's report, dated April 15, 1921, began with these words:

> *A controversy as to the location of the original discovery of gold, the third chronologically but the second of importance in what is now the state of Montana, has survived nearly two generations and the last of the party, Reginald (Bob) Stanley, died in London, England, nearly seven years ago. Additional interest is attached to this incident from the fact that he wore to his grave a ring made from some of the first gold taken from this discovery.*

The commission consulted with a number of early settlers still living and researched early histories and the earliest newspapers of the region, and acknowledged that "the great change in the contour of the locality made in improvements in the capital city...makes it difficult to designate exact sites."

Apparently unmoved by Watson Boyle's findings, Reginald Stanley's written and spoken testimony or even the opinions of geological or mining experts, the commission concluded its report in these words: "From the testimony presented there was little variance...The first gold was taken out near the intersection of Fuller Avenue and Sixth Avenue West, near the bed of the gulch from ground now occupied by the Montana Club Building."

On recommendation of the commission, an engraved bronze plaque, measuring thirty-two by forty inches, was subsequently created and bolted to the side of the building, where it remains today. With notable confidence, George L. Ramsey, chairman of the commission, wrote at the end of the official report, "We commend the design of the Historical and Pioneer societies of the state in finally settling this interesting controversy, and desire to testify that the labor and responsibility devolved on us has been a pleasure in its performance."

Gold Worth a King's Ransom

❧

by Ellen Baumler

Articles in this series, from time to time, have touched upon the function of that marvelous building at 206 Broadway, known to most of us simply as the "assay building." Its true *raison d'être*, and its historical significance have, for the most part, been buried with the passage of time. It seems a worthwhile project for an equally worthwhile building, to resurrect the reasons that put it there and delve into the amazing service it performed for almost sixty years.

When gold was discovered at Alder Gulch in 1863, Montana was part of the territory of Idaho. Even several years after the creation of the territory of Montana in 1864, the *Montana Post* lamented that immense quantities of gold bullion had found its way to the different United States' mints generally classified as "Idaho dust." A great deal of that had actually been taken from the placers of Montana. As politicians argued over where to establish a federal branch mint in the North-west, the *Montana Post* went on to state, "Through no spirit of jealousy or selfishness towards our neighbor, but from a prop-er sense of our just claims, we now assert that that Mint must come here, SOONER OR LATER...."

During the early days, the western miner faced a serious dilemma: how to render his gold into cash. He could take it himself to the federal mint at Philadelphia or he could pay exorbitant express tariffs to send it there and wait anxiously for weeks, even months, for the safe return of his currency. This was the course taken by Last Chance discoverer Reginald Stanley and his three companions, who sent some $170,000 worth of "securely boxed" gold dust down the Missouri River to Philadelphia via Forth Benton. Another option was to take the gold to the local banker, pay a heavy percentage and have it converted to cash on the spot. One prominent banker who specialized in buying gold dust was Henry Elling of Virginia City. He became one of the state's largest gold buyers and controlled seven Montana banks, including one in Helena. Elling was such an expert on the dust that he could tell by looking at

Under construction in 1875.

its color from exactly what diggings any given sample had been taken and estimate its value within a few cents. Selling to a private banker, although sometimes a necessity, left Uncle Sam a loser in the transaction. According to the *Weekly Herald* of April, 1868, it was "a conceded fact that the bulk of bullion falling into the bankers' hands of America" ultimately went to be coined in France or Great Britain. For these reasons and because Helena was the largest city near the headwaters of the Missouri, contemporaries argued that here would be the logical place to establish a branch mint.

The bill that was finally passed into law in 1874, however, established not a mint where currency was made, but a federal assay office, which was the next best thing. When the office opened in 1876-77, there were five other government assay offices, located in New York City, St. Louis, Charlotte (N.C.), Deadwood and Boise. Ground-breaking for the assay building took place in the summer of 1875 on land purchased by the government from C.L. Vawter. The cornerstone was laid with great ceremony in October by the Grand Lodge of Masons of Montana. Designed by Treasury Department architect A.B. Mullett and modified by his successor William Appleton Potter, the $75,000 building opened in January of 1877. It was the first recorded federal building in the territory of Montana (although the federal prison at Deer Lodge was built and in use by 1871, it became a state institution in 1889) and one of Helena's first permanent, multi-storied commercial buildings. Less than a decade later, some criticized the building's architectural style, calling it old-fashioned and lacking in good taste. It is true that the building, whose architecture was influenced by Gothic and Classical styles popular in the Midwest before the Civil War, showed no affinity with the blossoming Richardsonian Romanesque style displayed a few doors down in the new courthouse. Nevertheless, the "dignified little building" was like "Washington transplanted to the soil of Montana," and a source of great regional pride to its citizens.

MONTANA HISTORICAL SOCIETY

Charles Rumley was the first assayer and M.A. Meyendorf was the melter; both offices were by presidential appointment. In 1878 Russell B. Harrison (whose father, Benjamin Henry Harrison, was destined to become president in 1889) was appointed assayer, a position considered a choice political "plum" and one which he held until 1885. The elder Harrison, then a senator, claimed to have "sent 'the boy' out here to help win the West."

By 1900, the Helena Assay Office had purchased $30 million worth of gold bullion for Uncle Sam, all of it melted into gold bars worth a king's ransom in the stately building on Broadway. Miners both great and small brought their gold dust and nuggets to the Helena office which accepted amounts worth $50 or more.

The technical melting process was conducted on the first floor and the newly-made bars were then taken to the second-floor assay office. There a shearing machine cut triangular pieces from opposing corners of each bar. These two "clips" were flattened into sheets, the sheets cut into pieces and weighed. There were two assayers to one bar, each taking one of the clips. After weighing and figuring, if the assayers' results didn't match, the bar was sent back for remelting. The finished gold bar had a dark, dull richness, not a glittering finish. The office vault accommodated as much as $300,000 worth of bars at one time, and gold shipments were sent out weekly to the Philadelphia mint. In 1901, the *Anaconda Standard* boasted that there had never been a robbery at the assay office nor had any shipment ever been lost or stolen.

The precision of the office scales were a marvel. Carrie Strahorn writes of a tour she took through the "whole process of the works" in 1878. The scales were so sensitive that a pencil mark would change the balance: "I wrote my name on a piece of paper that had already been weighed and found the writing to add just $1/264$ of a grain."

A changing economy brought closure of the Helena Assay Office in 1934. The building was converted to apartments and so it remains today, under the proud ownership of Wanda Christofferson. Its outward appearance has changed very little since the 1870s. It was the old-fashioned architecture—unlike that of any other local building—that fueled its 1880s critics. But it is precisely that quality that has endeared it to Helenans in a later age. More important, however, is the very presence of this eye-catching building in Helena as a symbol of the great wealth that once came from Montana soil.

HELENA'S UNDERGROUND RIVER OF GOLD

ᘒᘒᘒ

BY DAVE WALTER

Since the 1860s, rumors have persisted that somewhere under Helena runs a rushing underground river of pure, clear, cold water. Moreover, the story goes, a gigantic rockslide off Mount Helena long ago diverted this ancient stream and left a dry, bedrock channel of gold-bearing gravels. Those gravels would produce incredible wealth—more than the original min-

ers took out of Last Chance Gulch—if only someone could find the old channel.

This persistent legend last surfaced in 1966, when a Helena writer caused a considerable stir with his research into the story. Helenans did not believe Charles D. Greenfield an irresponsible purveyor of fantasy. He had been born in the community in 1885 to a prominent newspaper family, and he had built a solid reputation.

Charles D. Greenfield

MONTANA HISTORICAL SOCIETY

In his youth, Greenfield worked for both Helena newspapers—the *Independent* and the *Montana Record-Herald*—and he covered nine legislative sessions for a network of Montana papers. In 1919 he took up farming in the valley, while serving in his father's office at the Montana Department of Agriculture and Publicity. From 1923 until his retirement in 1950, Charley worked as a home-office executive for the Montana Life/Western Life Insurance Company.

In retirement Greenfield served a term (1954-1960) as a Lewis and Clark County commissioner, continued as a school-board member in District #15, and worked as a state insurance examiner. During the 1960s and early 1970s, both he and his wife, Elizabeth Nelson Greenfield, wrote scores of newspaper and magazine articles on Western-history subjects. Of them all, Charley's piece entitled "Helena's Hidden Channel of Gold," which ran in the winter 1966 issue of *Old West* magazine, produced the greatest response.

During months of research in the Montana Historical Society's library/archives, Greenfield uncovered fragments of the "underground river" story. His article wove these pieces into a compelling argument that relied on two factors: (1) that a substantial underground river still flowed beneath the community; (2) that the river's abandoned streambed could be located.

As evidence, Greenfield first relates a story told in the 1864 placer-mining camp of Last Chance Gulch. Two miners who rushed to the Last Chance strike told of traveling through this area the previous year, pursued by a band of Blackfeet. After hiding for several days, they crossed at the head of the valley and discovered a fissure in the earth, a crevice large enough to hold a stagecoach. From this gap rose the sound of running water—an underground stream.

Since the opening revealed an inclined slope, one brave miner carefully descended the 100 feet to the stream. He returned with a shirtful of gravel, containing many flakes of gold. In 1864, while other miners worked the claims along Last Chance Creek, these two men searched for the unmarked fissure. Although they never did find it again, their persistence gave credence to their story of the "underground river."

Charles Greenfield is quick to caution his Doubting-Tho-

An early Helena placer mining operation.

mas readers about disappearing fissures in the Helena valley. He reminds them that several of these crevices had appeared during the earthquake series of 1935, some of them wide enough to hold an auto. Yet, within twenty-four hours, the chasms had closed, leaving no remains. Then Greenfield tells the story of Colonel George W. Keeler.

Keeler was a seasoned California miner who had devoted his life to finding Helena's "hidden channel of gold." During the winter of 1867-1868, Keeler was working a mine in Big Indian Gulch, about four miles south of the Last Chance settlement. That whole winter the camp buzzed about a rich strike made by two local merchants, Taylor and Thompson, on their claim in the lower Gulch (down the slope from North Main, between to-day's Fourteenth and Fifteenth streets, in the parking lot of Capital City Bowl). Tunneling through a layer of clay, Taylor and Thompson struck an immensely wealthy gravel—richer than anything found higher in the Gulch. That winter they took more than $1 million from ground well below the Last Chance bed-rock. Although the miners called their marvel a "pothole," Keeler doubted this designation, because he had encountered true "potholes" in California. Rather, he believed, the Taylor and Thompson strike had tapped into the channel of a "dead river."

Keeler had run into this "dead river" phenomenon in the California gold fields. It identified a streambed whose original channel long before had been blocked by a landslide, forcing the water into a new channel. California's "dead rivers" had proven bonanzas, and that promise pushed Keeler into action. The Colonel was convinced that the original river ran southeast to northwest at the head of the valley. So, starting in the late 1860s, he began to sink mine shafts in likely places.

In his first attempt, Keeler believed that he tapped the "old channel," since he recovered a surprising amount of heavy gold. Then, without warning, his drift (horizontal tunnel) and shaft filled with water. Although disappointed that he had wasted all his work, the prospector became even more convinced that his theory was sound.

Keeler sank a second hole nearby, with the same result. A family named Brooks used this shaft as a well for years.

A third and a fourth shaft also flooded out. Although he purchased a series of larger and larger pumps, Keeler's succeeding prospects suffered the same fate. One shaft, sunk on the northwest corner of Hauser and Park, became a stock well for neighbors.

Keeler periodically ran out of money and worked at other jobs to finance his prospecting. Year after year he persisted, sinking shafts, laying drains, refining his theory about the "hidden channel of gold." During the late 1880s, he moved his prospect holes to Helena's west side, into the Hauser and Cannon additions.

On these sagebrush slopes, he sank a series of four shafts. In each, however, he ran into a mass of slide rock that had torn loose from Mount Helena during some ancient age. The loose rock tumbled into the hole faster than he could remove it, and Keeler abandoned each attempt. Yet these failures reinforced his theory of an old landslide that changed the course of the original river.

Keeler's last shaft sat on the northwest corner of Knight Street and Madison Avenue (near the current site of the Lamplighter Motel). Its failure convinced him to move farther away from Mount Helena and to tunnel into the hill horizontally, under the layer of slide rock. With new funding from his brother, Keeler planned to begin his drift tunnel in the spring of 1891. On April 27 of that year, however, the Colonel died—and his quest died with him. The *Helena Independent* remarked (April 29, 1891):

> *Much of Keeler's acquired wealth was lost in his Hidden Gulch channel ventures....[Nevertheless] Colonel Keeler was one of the most sanguine of men. He believed that the precious metal was to be found in the bed of the underground river, and the only question was the way to get at it. His faith in the theory was evidenced by the amount of money he put in it.*

Besides the Keeler story, author Greenfield presents some additional evidence. He tells the tale of C.W. Clements, the dredgemaster on the Porter Brothers dredge that worked the gravels north of Custer Avenue and west of Montana Avenue. Clements reported a minimum of water for dredging until, at thirty-five feet below the surface, the dredge opened an underground water course.

The water flowed in rapidly and filled the pond. Then it displayed an even more remarkable quality: despite the tons of clay, dirt, and gravel that the dredge's conveyor belt continually dumped into the pond, the water remained blue and clear. Clements remarked, "You would only find this condition where there is a current with the water constantly changing." Clements became even more convinced that he had tapped an underground stream when the dredge moved to the east side of Montana Avenue. There the company had to buy well water from a nearby farmer just to keep the dredge afloat.

Early in the century, two ranchers near the Cooney Convalescent Home—one to the east and the other to the west—also contributed to the theory of an underground river. In both cases, the water-poor owners dug wells that released an abundance of fresh water, more than they could ever use in their ranch operations. Greenfield speculated that the ranchers had struck the same stream that surprised the Porter Brothers' dredgemaster.

Greenfield concludes his piece on "Helena's Hidden Channel of Gold" with two complementary stories. In the first, he tells of railroad workers who had reported "echoing underground rumblings" every time a train passed a spot southwest of the Lewis and Clark County Fairgrounds complex, near where the N.P. tracks turn north to begin their ascent of Mullan Pass.

In the second story, Greenfield quotes Dan Boyle, a Northern Pacific Railroad division superintendent. Boyle said that he always believed that an underground cavern lay between the N.P. depot at the end of Helena Avenue and the roundhouse. He declared, "Every time a locomotive passed between the two points there was a hollow underground rumbling. I was afraid that someday a locomotive simply would be swallowed up and disappear."

Controversy over Charley Greenfield's article ran through Helena early in 1966.

Over coffee and cafe lunches, proponents debated skeptics over the validity of the "underground river of gold." Greenfield simply observed:

The story of the Hidden Channel, with its legend of gold, will not die. ...There still are people who believe in the existence of the Hidden Channel, with its wealth of gold. They believe that sooner or later some enterprising firm or individual will find it and garner more than the $10 million that came out of Last Chance Gulch....Finding a fortune rarely comes easily, but I hope that—someday—someone will prove that George Keeler was right.

Rumors of Helena's "underground river of gold" now have circulated for more than 125 years. Adamant proponents and unshakable opponents of the theory still exist in our community. And the controversy will continue, for this type of get-rich-quick story has fueled gold prospecting throughout the West for centuries.

Remember: Get permission from the proper authorities before you begin to dig that shaft in your backyard or in the nearby public park!

JAMES WHITLATCH & THE LAST CHANCE MOTHERLODE

BY KIMBERLY MORRISON

James Whitlatch was twenty-one when he arrived in the Prickly Pear Valley during the fall of 1864, hoping to capture some of the gold splendor that was being panned from Last Chance Gulch in Helena. Although one of the youngest miners in the camp, founded by the "Four Georgians" in July 1864, the Pennsylvania native had an impressive background, highlighted by mining stints in Nevada and Idaho and his ownership of a gold mine in the Black Hawk Mining District of Colorado at the young age of sixteen.

By the time that Whitlatch reached Helena, the camp's gulches had already been scoured and claimed by hungry miners, leaving little ground for him to stake. Undaunted by the horde of men in Last Chance Gulch, Whitlatch wandered into the hills south of town a few weeks after his arrival with the intention of finding Helena's motherlode—the source of Last Chance Gulch's placer.

For several months, Whitlatch searched the gulches and hills south of town for the vein of quartz that supplied the rich diggings in Helena, but he returned to the camp each evening empty-handed. By January of 1865, Whitlatch and his partner Eli Wibley were somewhat discouraged by their unsuccessful hunting attempts, but they vowed to continue for another month. If they did not find Helena's motherlode by late February, they would leave the valley and return to more prosperous camps south of town.

Much like the "Last Chance" discovery by the Four Georgians, Whitlatch found Helena's motherlode at the end of February 1865, just days from the date targeted for abandoning his search. The lode was found in a granite deposit three and a half miles southwest of Helena in a divide between Oro Fino and Grizzly Gulches. Originally known as Owyhee

James Whitlatch.

Park, the site of the Whitlatch vein and its contiguous leads was quickly developed, and the Whitlatch-Union lode became the first discovery of gold-bearing quartz in southwestern Montana. By July of 1865, Whitlatch joined the ranks of the many self-made Montana millionaires who lavishly flaunted their success and power.

James Whitlatch did not waste any time putting his new-found wealth to work for him. He hosted Helena's first Fourth of July celebration at Owyhee Park in 1865. The enormous picnic and dance was purportedly attended by thousands from rag-tag miners to Helena's finest citizens. Whitlatch went to great lengths to impress his new neighbors, building a large dance pavilion and securing most of the champagne and wine in Helena specifically for the occasion. He is also credited with lending the Fisk brothers money to bring the *Montana Post* newspaper from Virginia City to Helena. The *Montana Post* became Helena's premier newspaper of the time, the *Helena Herald*. Whitlatch persuaded his attorney and good friend Wilbur Fisk Sanders to move his interests to Helena as well, bringing a number of prosperous ventures into the community and exploiting his own mining interests as well.

The Whitlatch-Union Mine and other claims in Owyhee Park were worked continuously throughout the spring and summer of 1865. Although thousands of dollars of surface ore were still visible, Whitlatch had exhausted the easily-extractable quartz in his mine by autumn. In late 1865, Whitlatch therefore sold a portion of his claim to the National Mining and Exploiting Company of New York, which immediately shipped machinery to the site and constructed a ten-stamp quartz mill. Other mining companies began developing the area, and by 1873 several stamp mills served the mines in Oro Fino Gulch. The Whitlatch-Union Mine and adjacent claims were the largest producers of gold bullion in the United States between 1871 and 1873. Over half of the gold taken from the mines between 1865 and 1890 was extracted during 1872 alone, when $3.5 million worth was produced.

With the Whitlatch-Union Mine and other nearby claims booming, the adjacent mining camp grew at a rapid pace. After the National Mining and Exploiting Company began operating the mines in 1865, Owyhee Park was briefly known as Roosevelt in honor of the two primary stockholders in the com-

The Whitlatch-Union Mine near Unionville, 1879.

THOMAS H. RUTTER PHOTOGRAPH, MONTANA HISTORICAL SOCIETY

pany, James and Theodore Roosevelt, relatives of our twenty-sixth president. Several saloons, a general store, a laundry and a number of small cabins and shacks were built. In 1867, the name of the camp was changed from Roosevelt to Unionville.

Unionville continued to thrive long after Whitlatch left the area for San Francisco in 1870. The early 1870s were the most prosperous years for the mines, which brought in roughly $6 million in gold. Unionville became home to almost 300 people, including three general merchants, three saloon keepers, a barber, a grocer, four boardinghouse keepers, a brewer, a Chinese laundryman, and a butcher who operated a nearby slaughterhouse. Local merchant P.C. Constans capitalized most successfully on the mining boom, establishing the largest general mercantile, a saloon, a few mines, and the camp's post office. In 1873, a nondenominational church/district schoolhouse was constructed by Superintendent S.J. Jones of the Owyhee mine, adding to the "permanent [and] pleasing appearance" of Unionville.

The bust of the boom town commenced in the 1880s when water began seeping into the mine shafts. In addition, the price of gold dropped significantly in the early 1890s, and miners began leaving Unionville in droves. The town's post office was discontinued in 1890, when the camp's population dropped below 100. Subsequently, the town's founder, James Whitlatch, distraught by the country's economy and several bad business decisions, committed suicide in a San Francisco hotel. The former Montana-made mining baron died a sad and penniless man at the same time as the mine and town he had founded was perishing. The Whitlatch-Union Mine closed in 1897, although other nearby claims continued to operate.

Many Montana mining camps survive only as derelict ghost towns, but Unionville was not abandoned. A small mining revival brought workers into the area in 1904 and the economic hardship and earthquake devastation in Helena during the 1930s encouraged families and squatters to move into Unionville and clean up the old buildings and cabins. Today, the small suburb has survived almost for over 130 years, and it is a quiet reminder of the mining boom that made Helena what it is.

THE FERRY IN
THE CANYON

BY CHERE JIUSTO

The settlement of Canyon Ferry, a place for crossing the turbulent Missouri River, was born in 1865. The river narrowed at this juncture, allowing a passage from the booming Last Chance mining camp and diggings west of the Missouri, to the rich gold fields in the gulches east of the river.

News of gold strikes spread like wildfire through the mining camps of Montana Territory during the 1860s. In late summer of 1864, just weeks after gold strikes by the "Four Georgians" at Last Chance Gulch, four other hopeful prospectors stumbled onto traces of gold to the east, across the Helena Valley and the Missouri River. Hunkered down on the flanks of the Big Belt Mountains, they dropped a prospect hole along one of the numerous creeks meandering into the Missouri from the Belts, and did not come up empty handed.

The miners quickly worked their way up the gulch, where the gold colors were richer, and laid claim to much of the canyon. Three of these prospectors were Southerners with Dixie still in their hearts, and they christened their bonanza Confederate Gulch.

Gold fevers ran high and traffic was heavy to such places as Confederate Gulch, White's Gulch, Magpie Gulch and Cave Gulch. Taking miners across to the gold fields east of the river became a brisk business at Canyon Ferry in 1865, when John Oakes established a ferry there. When Oakes sold his interest in the Canyon Ferry just one year later, the new ferryman, Capt. J.V. Stafford, built a hotel and store at the landing.

The ferry changed hands again, shortly thereafter, when Court Sheriff purchased the business. Sheriff had followed the gold strikes from Illinois to Helena by way of Wyoming in 1866. He first worked the mines in Diamond City, then hired on as a carpenter, to help build a wooden flume for the Magpie–Cave Hill ditch. In 1875 he opened a general mercantile to serve the miners in camps east of the Missouri River, at Cavetown, one of the first settlements in the area. He moved to nearby Canyon Ferry in 1880, and by 1883 had established a general store. Sheriff added a livery stable and two-and-a-half-story hotel— The Canyon House—at the landing. The Canyon House was well-appointed, with a grand piano in the parlor, and red-checked cloths draping tables in the dining room.

A stagecoach on the Missouri River ferry at Black Rock

Named for its location at the mouth of Black Rock Canyon, the cluster of log buildings called Canyon Ferry served as a center for mining and ranching in outlying flats and gulches around the Missouri River. Most of the gold in the district came in the form of shallow, placer deposits, which were mined out by the late 1870s. In the years that followed, farming and ranching became the mainstay of settlements clinging to the hem of the Big Belt Mountains.

The Canyon Ferry settlement was located seventeen miles out from Helena, making it a convenient stage stop on the Helena–White Sulphur Springs run. Until 1918, the Sheriff family ran a stage line and U.S. mail run on this route. Court Sheriff, local postmaster and stage manager, negotiated rugged mountain roadways across the Big Belts in the "Mud Wagon" stage (named for the often dismal road conditions). The stage departed Helena at 4:30 A.M., changed horses at Canyon Ferry, Diamond City and Fort Logan, and arrived in White Sulphur Springs at 7:30 in the evening. In the winter it was a two-day trip with an overnight stay at Diamond City. Sheriff's base at Canyon Ferry grew to include the Sheriff family home, post office, stage office, stage barn, saloon, hotel and a store.

At Canyon Ferry, the charge for being swept across the river on an open barge was two bits for a horse and rider, fifty cents for a team. It was one of several ferry crossings on the Missouri in the Helena Valley, and was the closest to the budding city of Helena. Others located downriver included Blake Ferry a few miles upriver, Pickering Ferry near Winston, and two ferries in the Townsend vicinity.

The completion of the first dam at Canyon Ferry in 1898 signalled the death of the ferry, for it left the waters below the dam too choppy for safe crossing. Those wishing to cross once again made the passage in rowboats, until the completion of a bridge in 1901.

Today the entire site is underwater. The second Canyon Ferry dam washed away the landing, and only the tiny graveyard on Cemetery Island peeks above the water, to mark the original ferry site at Black Rock Canyon.

EARTHQUAKE!

Why the Queen City Shakes, Rattles and Rolls

BY Chere Jiusto

*When we talk of history, a few thousand years is consid-
ered really ancient. But when we consider the history of the
earth and geologic events, we are talking about a time span
so long that our human brains have trouble fathoming it.*

*We live with those patterns of order, laid down so far in
the ancient past they predate human times by millions and
millions of years. And once in a while, those primordial forces catch us by surprise, at times creating something as won-
drous and beautiful as an artesian well, at other times shaking the very foundations of our everyday world.*

Tremors in the earth were nothing new to Helena in 1935;
native people had warned the first settlers in the Helena Valley
of frequent earthquakes and the years that followed proved
them right. So when a vigorous earthquake hit on October 3,
people didn't overly concern themselves.

The October 3 quake is now regarded as the first of a series
of 1935-1936 "felt" earthquakes, all strong enough to detect
without any seismic equipment and numbering over 2,000 by
June 30 of the following year. During this period of earthquake
"swarms" there were only two quake-free days, and some days
weathered many quakes.

On October 12, the greatest number were felt, one big one

and some thirty aftershocks. On October 18, the strongest quake was registered, lasting over a half minute and felt as far away as Spokane, Boise and Cody.

One reason for all this shaking reaches back to the formations of the West and the Rocky Mountains. Geologically young, and still moving, the Northern Rocky mountains are still rising, while the basins and valleys in between are falling. Helena is situated at the northern end of a corridor riddled with fault lines, where the mountains are pulling away from their sinking surroundings. The "intermountain seismic zone" is a corridor of extensive faulting and earthquake activity extending south from here, through Yellowstone, as far as the Wasatch Front around Salt Lake.

Geologists believe a main fault runs directly under the Helena (or Prickly Pear) Valley, making Helena an earthquake-prone place.

Once things start shaking, the reason that Helena rattles and rolls is because half the town has the bad fortune to rest upon glacial alluvium laid down during the late Pleistocene epoch (about 2 million years before present). During the Pleistocene ice ages, a giant ice sheet dammed the Missouri River near Great Falls, flooding the Helena Valley and laying down glacial sediments on the old lake bottom. Part of that ancient lakebed now comprises much of the Helena valley—a roughly circular area some 12 by 13 miles in dimension.

It is no wonder that the valley is such a prolific source of sand and gravel now. It is equally no wonder that when the valley—on those loose footings—starts to tremble, things start moving. Geologist David Alt, in *Roadside Geology of Montana* explained the situation this way:

> *Think of a large bowl full of soft pudding; the bowl simulating bedrock and the pudding the soft sediments. Then imagine yourself sharply tapping the edge of the bowl to simulate an earthquake. The pudding will move far more visibly than the bowl, and so will the valley sill sediments move more violently than the bedrock during an earthquake.*

The earthquakes of 1935-1936 hit hardest throughout the eastern portions of town atop valley sediments, and out into the valley itself. "In some sections of the city almost every chimney crashed to the ground and in practically every home in the east half of the city there was some damage ranging from slight plaster cracks to complete demolition," wrote local principal C.R. Anderson at the time.

With seismic technology of the day, geologists zeroed in on a farm some three miles northwest of town, which they believed lay directly over the Prickly Pear fault. The owner described the rolling of the earth like a dog shaking water off itself. Geologists have since said that had there been more development in the valley at the time, the 1935 earthquake damage would have been much greater.

A map prepared by Oscar Baarson, city engineer at the time, graphically shows the damage running through Helena's Sixth Ward, across the east side, and down Last Chance Gulch. Buildings higher up on the foothills and bedrock outcrops, the Montana Capitol, Carroll College or the West Side for instance, fared far better.

The earth beneath Helena has not stopped moving since then. And from time to time a tremor will rattle our windows as a reminder that a big one could, and likely will, occur again sometime. As Robert Switzer of Western Montana College noted in 1982, there is much evidence to suggest that a buildup of geologic tension will recur and that "its subsequent release will take many Montanans back to the fall of 1935."

SHAKY HISTORY

BY LEANNE
KURTZ

They've got Disneyland, Beverly Hills, the 49'ers, the Chargers, the Rams (oh, yeah, forget the Rams!), glamorous movie stars, trials-of-the-century, gangs, smog, fires, floods, and, of course, those bone-jarring earthquakes.

California has nothing on Montana. We've got the Bob Marshall Wilderness, the Swan Valley, the Blackfoot River, legendary skiing on uncrowded slopes, glamorous movie stars, a beautiful vista from nearly any perspective, and, of course, those bone-jarring earthquakes.

Nineteen ninety-five marked the 60th anniversary of the most notorious series of earthquakes ever to thunder through the Helena Valley. For a harrowing month in 1935, it seemed that stuff would never stay on shelves and camping on the front lawn became the norm. October 1935, however, was not the first time Helenans have felt the ground shift beneath their shoes.

The first Anglo description of a quake in Montana, penned, naturally, by some of the first Anglos to explore and document the Wild West, is dated July 4, 1805. These notes from the Lewis and Clark Expedition read,

> *Since our arrival at the [Great Falls of the Missouri], we have repeatedly heard strange noises coming from the mountains in a direction a little to the north of west. It is heard at different periods of the day and night, sometimes when the air is perfectly still and without a cloud, and consists of one stroke only, or of*

five or six discharges in quick succession. It is loud and resembles precisely the sound of a six-pounder piece of ordnance at the distance of three miles. The solution of the mystery, given by the philosophy of the watermen, is that [the sound] is occasioned by the bursting of the rich mines of silver within the bosom of the mountain.

Sixty-four years later, Reverend D.S. Tuttle, a missionary bishop, and his family were eating breakfast at their home on Jackson Street in Helena when their repast was suddenly disrupted. Rev. Tuttle likened the sound to a heavy wagon dragged rapidly across a bridge and thought that perhaps a fast-moving freight wagon had collided with the corner of the family's house.

Mrs. Tuttle and her mother exclaimed that "some great piece of furniture has fallen somewhere." Apparently the tremor was not terribly traumatic or frightening, as the Tuttle family promptly resumed their breakfast and calmly discussed the possible sources of the curious noise. Rev. Tuttle wrote, "Soon after, I went down Main Street and discovered that the same disturbance had been noted everywhere. We were then sure the town had been visited by an earthquake."

Great pieces of furniture began falling and freight vehicles began running amok again in December of 1872. On December 12, 1872, The *Helena Weekly Herald* reported: "At 4:40 o'clock P.M. yesterday afternoon, 10th inst., and at 7 o'clock A.M. today, Helena was treated to the novelty of several earthquake shocks. The quaking was experienced in all parts of the city alike, and was accompanied by a rumbling noise, resembling that of a heavy freight train rumbling though our streets....The massive granite building in which the *Herald* office is located, shook as violently as the framework of a gaunt Hoosier, assailed by a fit of Wabash ague."

All right then, get the picture? Apparently two rather violent quakes shook most of southwestern Montana that afternoon, each lasting about five seconds. Mary G. Daugherty, then a student at St. Vincent's Academy, later wrote to her brother, David Hilger, of these tremors that a quick prayer at the onset of the shaking by the sister in charge alleviated academy students' fear and panic. When she returned home from school that day, Mary's mother recounted how her sewing machine kept inching away from her until she became frightened enough to grab the kids and run outside.

Helenans experienced comparatively minor quakes in the 1880s, 1890s and early 1900s. The next big one, though, wreaked havoc on buildings, injured two people, and jarred residents of Three Forks, Manhattan and Helena on June 27, 1925. The earthquake originated at Clarkston, near Three Forks at 6:23 P.M., but was felt by people as far away as southern Alberta, Cody, Wyoming, and Glasgow, Montana. Portions of brick buildings collapsed in Willow Creek and Manhattan and a 40,000-ton rock slide blocked rail traffic for weeks near Lombard on the Missouri River. This tremor and the aftershocks which followed caused wells in the Helena area to dry up, created new springs, and increased the flow of hot springs at Alhambra and White Sulphur Springs. Chimneys in Helena crumbled from the vibrations and residents ran into the streets to escape any falling debris.

In Missoula, a jury was in the middle of deliberations when they felt two sharp jolts. "We sure didn't waste any time agreeing upon a verdict after that second tremor," one juror was quoted as saying.

As damaging and unnerving as they may have been, the earthquakes in the Helena area leading up to those of October 1935 pale in comparison. Although the human toll has been slight in Helena's major quakes, the property destruction left in the wake of over a century of temblors continues to be a sobering reminder of how easily our carefully-crafted structures can crumble around us.

The Quakes of '35

BY JON AXLINE

*One can get used to about anything except the solid
earth shaking constantly. Only the pioneering spirit
of the early founders that is still retained by the present
generation keeps the city from being a wilderness. If
Congressional Metals of Honor were given to groups
for outstanding courage, this community would deserve one.*

The Boston Globe, *1935*

In October 1935, Helena experienced perhaps the most
traumatic event in its short history. The October earthquakes
left an indelible mark on the city's residents and its buildings.
Memories of the earthquakes are still quite vivid for those who
weathered them. For those of us who are too young to have
experienced the event, the scars the quakes left on many of
Helena's buildings are still visible. Though the earthquakes lasted only seconds, they caused about $4 million in damage to
Helena and East Helena, resulted in four deaths, and forever
changed the city's appearance.

At 8:04 P.M. on October 18, 1935, Helena was rocked by a
strong portent of what was to come two hours later. The fore-
shock was the latest in a series of tremors that had been plagu-
ing Helena since October 3. Seismologists understood little of
the phenomenon and felt that it was the earth merely "settling
down." Many Helenans, apparently, felt the same way as the
rumbling died away. At 9:47 P.M., however, the city was struck
by a Magnitude-6 earthquake that was both stronger and longer than anything previously experienced.

The site of one of the October 18 quake's fatalities.

The epicenter of the earthquake was about four miles northeast of Helena at Burt Lichtward's ranch on Canyon Ferry Road. Observers in the city noted that although the quake's greatest intensity was from east to west, there was also a strong vertical and twisting motion. One man reported that the walls and floors of his apartment "seemed to be going in and out, and up and down, as if the room was a large bellows."

When the quake struck, many Helenans fled their homes or businesses to avoid being trapped and killed. Those more level-headed, however, remained indoors. Most of the reported injuries were caused by falling brick and plaster and broken glass. David Harris was killed when a brick building façade collapsed on him on South Main Street; Charles Siggelink was slain by falling brick and timber when he fled a building used as a transient camp at the fairgrounds.

The earthquake knocked out the city's electrical power, yet, surprisingly, the gas and water mains did not rupture. When the shaking finally ceased, the darkness was broken only by the sound of falling brick and plaster and by the flashlights and automobile headlights that pierced the dust-laden gloom. Driven out of their homes, people huddled together in front yards or vacant lots; many built bonfires to keep warm. Others salvaged what they could from their homes. Although the police and National Guard quickly mobilized to prevent looting, Helena's streets were soon congested by those who sought to survey the damage and check on friends and relatives. One witness described the atmosphere in Helena that night as "surreal."

Fortunately, neither of Helena's two hospitals sustained major damage and were able to treat the hundred or so people who sought aid (only twelve cases were treated and released). Many others sought treatment at the city's pharmacies. The collapse of a warehouse's wall onto a freight car loaded with whiskey afforded comfort of a different sort for those willing to retrieve it (this was Helena's only known case of looting that night).

As the night progressed, Helena was continuously shaken by aftershocks, which prevented many from returning to their homes. Instead, front yards and vacant lots became makeshift campgrounds. Others slept in their cars or in garages. In one instance, nineteen people crowded into a one-car garage. Children from the Deaconess Home spent several nights at a local dance hall called "The Shanty." Anxiety, however, prevented most Helenans from sleeping much that night.

When dawn broke, the extent of the damage to Helena could easily be seen. The areas of Helena situated on bedrock were relatively unscathed, while those areas built on underlying alluvial or glacial soil were seriously damaged. The west end was largely intact, whereas the south central district was not so fortunate. Portions of the Sixth Ward were devastated and the neighborhoods between Montana Avenue and Main Street sustained severe damage. The newly opened high school (now the Helena Middle School) was partially destroyed; the once straight chalk lines at the adjacent Vigilante Stadium were made wavy by the quake.

Although largely built on old placer tailings, most of the buildings on Last Chance Gulch remained structurally intact, though there was an abundance of fallen brick and broken glass littering the sidewalks and street. The more recently constructed buildings on the Gulch fared the best. Many of the older buildings, which lacked steel or concrete frames or were poorly constructed, suffered the most. The state capitol, St. Helena Cathedral, and the City-County Building sustained little damage. At the Civic Center, the sole spire remained intact, while the county courthouse's clock tower was totalled.

Damage to residences consisted primarily of cracked and collapsed brick walls, toppled chimneys and cracked plaster. About 10 percent of the 300 houses inspected by City Engineer Oscar Baarson were destroyed or later razed. The earthquake contributed to an already severe housing shortage in the Capital City.

Other buildings seriously damaged included the gymnasium at the Intermountain Union College (now the Department of Corrections and Human Services across from Capital Hill Mall), the old high school, the Northern Pacific and Great Northern Railway depots, the Florence Crittenton Home and St. Joseph's Orphanage.

After the earthquake, City Engineer Baarson inspected damaged buildings and issued Certificates of Occupancy for those deemed to be safe. In all, he inspected 3,500 buildings, over half of which sustained some degree of damage. The day after the quake, the City Council passed an ordinance forbidding all public gatherings until Baarson inspected the buildings.

Although many Helenans may have thought the danger had passed with the October 18 quake, they were once again reminded of nature's violence only fourteen days later. At 11:37 on the bitterly cold morning of October 31, the city was again shaken by a Magnitude-6 earthquake. Although it was less severe than the October 18 event, people were better able to observe its effects because it occurred in the daylight. For instance, people in "downtown streets reported seeing five- and six-story buildings sway far out into the street above their heads." The earthquake lasted only nineteen seconds, but it administered the coup de grace to many of the buildings damaged two weeks earlier.

This time, damage to St. John's Hospital forced the facility to evacuate its patients. Bryant and Hawthorne schools, Carroll College, old St. Paul's Methodist Church and the county poor farm sustained major damage. The new high school was further damaged by fire. Both the Fire and the Police departments evacuated their headquarters—the Police Department maintained law and order from its single paddy wagon until new quarters were found.

The Sixth Ward, Main Street and Ninth Avenue sustained serious damage, forcing the police to rope off portions of the streets to prevent injuries from falling debris (many were already afraid to venture downtown in the wake of the first quake).

At the Kessler Brewery, two men were killed while repairing damage caused by the first earthquake; they were thrown from the smokestack and buried in rubble. Many buildings heavily damaged by the first earthquake sustained even more damage, eventually forcing their abandonment or demolition.

In the aftermath of both earthquakes, disaster relief agencies and civic and church organizations quickly rallied to the aid of the community. The Red Cross conducted a door-to-door survey of damage to the residential areas and gave assistance to 422 families. Nearly 95 percent of the $86,640 spent by the Red Cross in Helena went to the rehabilitation of damaged homes.

The Salvation Army established a refugee camp at Green Meadow Ranch for those who could not return to their homes. They received donations of cots, mattresses, blankets, heating stoves and money from the Red Cross, Federal Emergency Relief Administration and from people all over Montana.

Because the earthquakes rendered the new high school unusable, both the Great Northern and the Northern Pacific railroads loaned the city several railcars for use as classrooms. The School Board reported that attendance at the "High School on Wheels" was 85 percent of normal when classes reopened on December 16.

Within a year, nearly two thirds of the damage caused by the earthquakes had been repaired. The city experienced 2,218 aftershocks, but Helenans were optimistic that the worst was over.

A Nerve-Wracking Week

By Ellen Baumler

Nearly every individual had some specific experience to relate, whether it was one of pathos or humor.... Whatever it was it added a personal touch to the general vibrating of the earth.

C.R. Anderson and M.P. Martinson
in *Montana Earthquakes*, 1936

On the evening of October 3, 1935, Fred and Juanita Buck noticed that the pictures on the walls of their home at 531 Fifth Avenue moved slightly and dishes in the cupboards tinkled. The event was forgotten until nine days later in the wee morning hours of October 12, when a severe jolt "shook the house until the walls seemed to be weaving in all directions." Within minutes, Helena homes were emptied and the entire population was out in the streets. Fred wrote that no one needed to ask, "Was that an earthquake?"

The town had sustained only very minor damage, but during the six days that followed, small tremors continued to set the town on edge. In retrospect Fred wrote that the jolt of the 12th proved to be "hardly a cocktail to a dinner." Like many other Helenans, the Buck family's packed bags and bedrolls stood ready during that nerve-wracking week. On Wednesday night the 16th, the earth suddenly fell deathly still; most felt this was a bad omen. Nevertheless at noon on the 18th, Fred retrieved the bags from the car and piled them back in the house in spite of Juanita's protests. A similar scenario was no doubt enacted in countless Helena households.

Fred Buck and his office force at the State Water Conservation Board had been putting in long hours on Public Works Administration loans and grants and handling the Work Projects

Administration program. That Friday night, October 18, Fred was in his office on the second floor of the Montana Block with six engineers going over plans for a storage dam. There had been one severe jolt just after dinner. The peculiar dead calm which followed intensified nervous anticipation. At 9:47 the crash came:

> *We jumped out of our chairs but could not stand up....The noise alone of grinding brick and groaning timbers, the rattling windows, and the roar of the quake itself, were enough to terrify one to say nothing of being jostled about like a lone marble in a tomato can. About that time the plaster began showering from the walls and ceiling, and in the midst of it all the lights went out. There we were trying to stay on our feet while being swatted with falling plaster in the ghastly darkness....As soon as the worst was over, we struck matches to pick our way thru the dark halls over plaster and down the stairs to the street. The earth and building were still trembling. The choking dust that filled the air was as thick as a heavy fog....People were running as though they were insane;...the streets were alive with cars; and the weird yellow cast of headlights piercing the thick blanket of dust was un-canny.*

When Fred arrived home, Juanita and four-year-old Mary were uninjured, but their home was split on all four sides and full of debris. Juanita's foresight and subsequent quick exit, mirrored in homes all over town, proved that anxiety played a major role in keeping the population on its toes and ready to jump. But luck, or perhaps providence, had a lot to do with it too.

Students at the new Helena High School were in the auditorium rehearsing a play. The teacher seemed to sense that something was about to happen and dismissed the class. Just moments after the last student vacated the building, the quake struck and debris crashed onto the stage.

At St. Vincent's Academy, the girls were getting ready for

Merchandise lost in the October 18 earthquake.

bed when the earth began its violent shakes. Sisters Eugenia Donnelly, Helena Fisher and Maurita Postlewait told the girls to dress quickly and, carrying candles, led them down the dark stairs. At someone's shouted suggestion, they bypassed the first doorway and continued down the stairs to a different exit just as they heard the wall fall and block the doorway not taken: "When daylight came, it was found that the Sisters and girls had providentially been guided over live wires and breaches in construction work...."

During the next thirteen days, people lived in tents all over town; aftershocks were continuous. Visitors flocked to Helena to see the damage, and had only to stay less than an hour to feel a good tremor. Restaurants emptied in a second, with patrons not returning to finish or pay for their meals. When the earth again became still on the 30th, many took it for a bad sign. The final big one struck on Halloween, at 11:37 in the morning. Even though it struck with equal intensity, daylight made it not quite so terrifying.

In the aftermath of the quakes, numerous accounts proved that Helena did not lose its sense of humor. Fred Buck titled

Life goes one during the aftershocks following the largest earthquake.

his account "The Narrative of how the Bux became Quakers." Similarly, the newspaper tells of a woman who was making jelly when the Friday night quake came. A flatiron was the first thing that fell into the vat; it was followed by the ironing board. Later, a volunteer tiptoed in to shut off the gas and slipped on the kitchen floor, falling right into—you guessed it—the jelly!

C.R. Anderson (then principal at Broadwater and Hawthorne schools) relates how two cars were traveling toward each other seventeen miles outside Helena. The Missouri River was on one side of the road and a steep cliff on the other. The cars were a short distance apart when a major temblor sent huge boulders and dirt onto the roadway between them. There was nothing to be done except exchange keys and cars—which they did—and each went on his way.

Several new jokes also lightened the grim situation. It was said that hunters noticed that ducks flying in the vicinity preferred to take the long way around Helena. They would approach, circle and exclaim, "Quake, quake," and fly on.

And then there was the rumor that Helena had been renamed "Lena," not because it leaned, but because during that long October of 1935, earthquakes shook the "Hel" out of it!

THE NIGHT OF THE BIG GAME

BY HARRIETT C. MELOY

October 18, 1935. Al Lundborg, Lew Chittim, Freddy Ranf and Roland "Fuzzy" Ortmayer played football for Intermountain Union College that day; "Fuzzy" carried the ball for the fourth-period touchdown that won the game, 6-0, against Montana School of Mines. They played in Helena, on the field east of the IUC gymnasium on the site now occupied by the Capital Hill Mall. Intermountain's win over the Butte Orediggers was the first recorded in a long series of contests between the two colleges. Tension ran high during the game. At one time fists flew, bringing the Helena police to the field. Intermountain's hard-won victory was the first of two historic events on that 1935 October day.

After the stunning victory, about 200 students, faculty, and friends, gathered for a dance in the gymnasium. Even the most reluctant dancers, energized by the day's excitement, soon circled the floor.

At 9:50 P.M., six injured players sitting near the west wall of the building heard a deep rumble—announcing the first quake in a series of quakes that recurred in Helena over the next five months or more. A few moments later, the dancers also felt a second rumble, which marked the onset of the area's most violent earthquake.

At 9:52, before the lights went out, the brick walls of the

new gymnasium swayed in and out, like sides of a large empty packing box in a windstorm. Then all the lights went dark. The stunned crowd stood silent in the inky blackness. Then, voices murmuring and feet shuffling, the crowd moved quickly and quietly out of doors. Apprehension gripped the crowd; just as the light died they glimpsed a hole in the wall on the west side of the gym. Above the low talking and moving feet, a voice assured worried friends that most of the west wall bricks had fallen outside, that everyone was safe.

I vividly recall the warm air and the black night that enveloped us as we filed out the south door of the gym. I remember gazing down Butte Avenue to Montana Avenue where my two-story home was, and worrying about my family. My father was away; and my mother was home alone with two sisters and a brother. Had the old brick house withstood the quake? Fortunately, my date, A.J. Kempenar, offered to walk home with me to see how my family fared.

Our home at 815 Montana appeared intact. Later, however, we discovered that the heavy, stone-encased windows in the dining room were so shaken out of their casings that daylight appeared through the cracks.

Telephone lines were still operating and the Lymans, Mabel and Ranney, invited us over to spend the night in tents on their lawn on Peosta Street. By the light of flickering candles my mother and my siblings packed suitcases to move to the Lymans', where tents were being erected. It seemed safer for us to remain outdoors.

After driving my family across town, my date and I returned to the campus where a group of IUC men had just returned from celebrating the day's victory by lighting the "I" on Mount Ascension (a tradition observed after every winning game). The celebrants described seeing a flash across the sky, at about 10:00 P.M., as city lights disappeared, rocks rolled down hill and trees swayed. The men told of scrambling down the steep path in the night's blackness, and running to the campus to find, with relief, that classmates were safe.

Near midnight, several students carried mattresses from Mills Hall, to sit on while they watched a parade of automobiles exiting Helena (moving slowly—bumper to bumper). Ironically, others were heading into the city to view the destruction.

Eager to learn more about the results of the quake, several students suggested walking toward Main Street to observe the damage. My date and I joined them. We didn't feel the continuous quakes when walking. Lights glowed in houses along Broadway as we passed en route to the city center. At the end of Broadway, National Guardsmen informed pedestrians that the entire length of Main Street was barricaded. Militia patrolled the streets to warn unauthorized personnel away from tall buildings. They told us of the death of a man who was caught by a shower of brick as he ran from a building on South Main.

Leaving the battle-like scene of Last Chance Gulch, we strolled back to the college campus. We stopped for a few minutes to sit on the low stone wall surrounding the Court House. The earth still shook. How strange the sensation of sitting on solid granite yet feeling the earth shake under us. No one considered the danger of the tall Court House tower that might tumble at any moment.

While we classmates talked about the events of the evening, we speculated that the earthquake might change the course of our lives. What would be the fate of 200 college students if IUC were unable to finance the restoration of damaged buildings and continue?

Intermountain College did leave Helena soon after the quakes. It moved to Great Falls, and eventually became a part of Rocky Mountain College in Billings. Students dispersed to various other higher education institutions.

Most Helenans have forgotten the little college east of the city. But those attending Intermountain on that October night long ago, will never forget the school, the football game, and the earthquakes of 1935.

Just ask Al, Lew, Freddy—or me!

INDEX

Jon Axline, a Montana native, can trace his roots in Helena, through the Adami family, back to 1872. As a cultural resource specialist/historian for the Montana Department of Transportation, he has had the opportunity to visit many of the places—famous, infamous and less well known—where Montana's history was made.

Ellen Baumler, a Kansas native, taught for ten years in Tucson, Arizona, before moving to Helena in 1988. With a Ph.D. in medieval studies and three summers of co-directing a field school in Italy, she now takes delight in the accessibility and relevance of Helena's history. Ellen coordinates Montana's National Register of Historic Places sign program at the State Historic Preservation Office.

Chere Jiusto came to Helena from upstate New York in 1976. A historian for the Historic Preservation Office of the Montana Historical Society, she directed the study of Helena's oldest historic districts. She is also a ceramic artist and a former resident of the Archie Bray Foundation.

Leanne Kurtz is a Helena native and fourth-generation Montanan with ancestral ties to the tiny Tobacco-Root hamlet of Pony. She earned a bachelor's degree in history at Montana State University and is about halfway toward a journalism master's degree at The University of Montana . Leanne is currently employed as a research analyst for the Montana Legislative Services Division.

Harriett C. Meloy came to Helena in the early 1930s. She is active in many local and state organizations. She was on the staff of the Montana Historical Society library from 1957 to 1977. She also served on the original board of the Lewis and Clark County Historical Society.

Kimberly Morrison is a fourth-generation Montanan. A graduate student at the University of Oregon, she received her B.A. in history from the University of Montana in 1993. She worked as a historian and community surveyor for the Montana Historic Preservation Office. After a thirty-month study of Anaconda, she is an avid social and labor history buff.

Vivian A. Paladin, a native of Glasgow, has lived in Helena since 1956. A newspaper typesetter, reporter and editor since high school days, she was asked by K. Ross Toole to join the editorial staff of *Montana: The Magazine of Western History* in 1958. As associate editor and then for a dozen years editor, she saw the journal become a publication notable for solid historical content and high degree of pleasing design and readability.

Richard B. Roeder was a noted historian and professor emeritus at Montana State University. He was twice honored as the recipient of the Montana Award in the Humanities (1984 and 1988). With many publications to his credit, Rich was probably best known as the co-author of the definitive history of the state, *Montana: A History of Two Centuries*. He died in 1995.

Dave Walter is a Montana historian, researcher, writer, editor, and teacher. Since 1979 he has worked at the Montana Historical Society in Helena, where he currently serves as the society's Research Historian. Dave is the author of three books and scores of articles on the history of Montana and the West.